T0329377

GOVERNMENT
CONTROL IN WAR

GOVERNMENT CONTROL IN WAR

By

THE RIGHT HONOURABLE
LORD HANKEY
G.C.B., G.C.M.G., G.C.V.O., F.R.S.

With a Foreword by
G. M. TREVELYAN
Master of Trinity College

LEES KNOWLES LECTURES, 1945

CAMBRIDGE
AT THE UNIVERSITY PRESS
1945

CAMBRIDGE
UNIVERSITY PRESS

University Printing House, Cambridge CB2 8BS, United Kingdom

Published in the United States of America by Cambridge University Press, New York

Cambridge University Press is part of the University of Cambridge.

It furthers the University's mission by disseminating knowledge in the pursuit of
education, learning and research at the highest international levels of excellence.

www.cambridge.org
Information on this title: www.cambridge.org/9781107666504

First published 1945
First paperback edition 2014

A catalogue record for this publication is available from the British Library

ISBN 978-1-107-66650-4 Paperback

CONTENTS

Foreword: BY THE MASTER OF TRINITY   *page* 7

Introduction   9

Chapter I. PRINCIPLES   11
Government Control or Military Control?—The Government and Strategy
—Relations with Commanders-in-Chief—German Experience—The Prime
Minister's Responsibility—The Prime Minister and War Preparation.

Chapter II. PREPARATION BEFORE 1914   22
The Committee of Imperial Defence—The Phase of Principle—The Phase
of Policy—The Phase of Plans and Preparations—Empire Co-operation—
Position in 1914—Reason for Small Army—Traditional Peace Policy—
Conclusion.

Chapter III. THE GREAT WAR 1914–18   32
Government Control at Home—Secrecy—The War Council—The Dar-
danelles Committee—The War Committee—The War Cabinet—The
Secretariat—The Imperial War Cabinet—The Supreme War Council—
Earl Lloyd George.

Chapter IV. BETWEEN THE WARS   51
Administrative Preparation—Ancillaries to Air Warfare—Policy and Plan-
ning—The Air Ministry and R.A.F.—The Chiefs of Staff Committee—The
Secretariat—The Imperial Defence College—Observations.

Chapter V. THE PRESENT WAR   60
Government Control at Home—Military Control—Administrative Con-
trol—The Empire and Commonwealth—Inter-Allied Co-operation—
Political Control—Observations.

Chapter VI. SOME CRITICISMS EXAMINED   71
The 'Pernicious Committee System'—A Combined General Staff—The
Human Factor.

Chapter VII. THE FUTURE   78
Principles—Methods—Additional Conclusions—Back to the Committee
of Imperial Defence—Science and Engineering—Unpreparedness—The
Causes—Suggestions examined—Public Opinion—Histories and Memoirs
—The Universities—An Allegory.

Bibliography   89

FOREWORD

IT is quite unnecessary that I, or anyone else, should write a Foreword to introduce a work by Lord Hankey on his own subject. But it is his special request that I should do so, and I am the Master of the College that provides the Lees Knowles Lectures.

I call it his own subject, because for nearly forty years he has taken a leading part in the rapid development of the various organs of our modern Government Control in War, and knows better than anyone the inside working of the machinery of War Cabinets, Imperial Conferences, Councils and Service Committees which has been created with such success to win both the last and the present war.

Starting life as a Marine officer, 'soldier and sailor too', he became Assistant Secretary of the Committee of Imperial Defence, 1908, Secretary of that body, 1912–38, Secretary of the War Cabinet and Imperial War Cabinet, 1916–19, Secretary of the Cabinet, 1919–38, Clerk of the Privy Council, 1923–38, Secretary of the Imperial Conference and of many International Conferences between the two wars, Minister without Portfolio in the War Cabinet, 1939–40, Chancellor of the Duchy of Lancaster, 1940–41, Paymaster General, 1941–42, Chairman of the Scientific Advisory Committee and Engineering Advisory Committee, 1942–43— and very much else besides! As the first Secretary that the Cabinet ever had, he has seen from inside the important constitutional development of that body from a meeting of the King's confidential servants without minutes or secretariat, into a fully equipped council of state. And if any single man knows the government machinery by which the wars of this country and empire are organised, it is the author of these lectures. This little book is, therefore, an important contribution to our constitutional history as well as to the history of the two world wars.

G. M. TREVELYAN

INTRODUCTION

THE late Sir Lees Knowles, from whom these lectures take their name, was, like myself, an Old Rugbeian, and it was an especial pleasure for me to be the first lecturer to come from the same school as the founder.

It was also a privilege to deliver the lectures under the chairmanship of the Master of Trinity, who has made an inestimable contribution to our knowledge of history.

When first asked to choose a subject, my choice fell on 'Amphibious Warfare', in which, as a former officer of the Royal Marine Artillery, I had always taken a deep interest, and which has developed so remarkably during the present war. But here I found that my old friend Admiral of the Fleet Lord Keyes, who has much greater practical experience of the subject than I in this war and the last, had anticipated me in 1943.

I therefore fell back on a subject with which I have been identified since I became Assistant Secretary of the Committee of Imperial Defence in 1908 and Secretary in 1912.

The following chapters do not contain any sensational revelations. The facts are all to be found in published works. But they are widely scattered in official Blue Books, White Papers, Reports of Royal Commissions or Official Committees, Reports of debates in Parliament (Hansard), Official Histories, of which there must already be nearly fifty volumes, and, above all, in the Memoirs and personal diaries of the leading figures of the last war, at home and abroad. A list of the works actually consulted is given at the end of this book, but is only a fraction of the complete bibliography.

All that is attempted here is a brief synopsis of the development of Government Control from the establishment of the Committee of Imperial Defence at the beginning of the present century up to the date of the last lecture of the series (9th March 1945), to establish some basic principles, and to draw from the past some lessons for the future.

In pursuance of this theme, Chapter I is of an introductory character, in which an attempt is made to formulate a series of fundamental principles on which Government Control in War should be based. In subsequent chapters these are tested by an examination of the development of Government Control over the preparations for the Great War 1914-18 (Chapter II); during that war (Chapter III); between the two wars (Chapter IV); and in the present war (Chapter V). In the penultimate Chapter VI certain criticisms of the present system are examined, and the last chapter contains a summary of the existing principles and practice in Government Control in War followed by some suggestions for the future.

The 'Government Control' with which these chapters deal is the higher control of all the forces of a State, an Empire or an Alliance in a major war; the combination for the prosecution of the war of all the resources, both military and civil, of the States concerned; the methods and machinery by which, in the light of modern experience, especially in this war and the last, they can best be focused on the main task of defeating the enemy; and more particularly the principles on which the system should be founded.

Those 'controls' of such matters as food, fuel, lighting, transport, etc., which some people find exasperating are not part of the subject. They are part of the contribution which we all make to the national war effort, and, in the aggregate, are of considerable importance, but they are not dealt with here.

It will be convenient to mention, in order to avoid misunderstanding, that when the word 'military' is used, it refers to all three Fighting Services—Navy, Army and Air Force.

CHAPTER I

PRINCIPLES

A PRELIMINARY point of principle which confronts us at the outset is whether the whole of the control of war should not be delegated by the Government to the military authorities; in other words, whether a war should be controlled by statesmen or solely by fighting men.

GOVERNMENT CONTROL OR MILITARY CONTROL?

It was sometimes argued in the last war that as war is a matter of fighting, the proper method for its control is to choose the best possible military leaders and to leave the whole business to them.

That is a short-sighted view. It is, of course, true that the actual victory is brought about by the application of force. But the conduct of operations by sea, land or air is a very technical business, which requires the whole of the energies both of the General Staffs at home and of the leaders in the various theatres of war. Those leaders can only carry it out effectively if their forces are properly equipped and supplied, and on the assumption that all the material and moral resources of the nation are organised behind them. To do that the military leaders have neither the knowledge nor the time.

Very occasionally, it is true, a military leader has been thrown up who had the capacity to fulfil the dual role. Such was the Duke of Marlborough, who—to quote the Master of Trinity— 'acted as the head of the State in war-time for all military and diplomatic affairs, but he left to his colleagues the management of Parliament'.* Such a one also was Napoleon, who combined military, political and administrative gifts in a marked degree. But it was too big a job, even for Napoleon. In the long run he

---

* G. M. Trevelyan, *History of England*, p. 510.

over-reached himself, bled his country white, failed to appreciate
sea power, made a gigantic mistake in under-rating the intrinsic
strength of Russia, and brought his country down with a crash.
If the job was too big for Napoleon, it is infinitely larger to-day
owing to the huge increase in populations and fighting forces and
the complexity of modern life and Government. One of Hitler's
greatest mistakes has been his attempt to combine control of the
German war effort with constant interference with operations,
e.g. at Stalingrad, the Falaise 'pocket' in Normandy, and on many
other occasions. His country, too, is about to crash.

In a country like our own, governed by a Parliamentary system,
however, the arguments against military control are overwhelming.

Under the King the country is governed by a Parliament
elected by the people, and the House of Commons has the
responsibility of voting or refusing supplies. Whether in peace
or war the Government of the day, composed (with rare excep-
tions in times of war) of members of one or other House of
Parliament supporting the party or combination of parties pos-
sessing a majority in the House of Commons, has to persuade
Parliament, and especially the House of Commons, that its policy
is right so that supplies will be voted. That is a highly technical
business involving an intimate grasp of the whole machinery of
Government, for which no professional sailor, soldier or airman
is trained, or would care, to undertake responsibility. Indeed,
after the last war Sir William Robertson went so far as to express
the considered opinion that 'war is not so much a matter for
soldiers and sailors as soldiers and sailors sometimes think', and
even that—

The war afforded no confirmation of the view sometimes expressed
that the War Minister ought to be a professional soldier. *

* *Soldiers and Statesmen*, vol. I, p. 189.

THE GOVERNMENT AND STRATEGY

Of course, in the grand strategy of the war the views of the Service Chiefs must usually prevail. Even in this field, however, the last word must rest with the statesmen who are responsible for policy. They alone have full knowledge of the resources of the nation or alliance of nations at any given moment, and of the probable reaction of this or that operation on hesitant neutral nations. It is they who have to distribute the resources of their country in the manner best calculated to win the war. That is often a difficult matter to decide and mistakes can easily be made. If too much is allotted to the Navy, there may be too little left for the Army and the Air Force and *vice versa*. In the last and in the present war, for example, when at first we were preoccupied with the expansion of the Army and its supplies which, at the outset of both wars, were totally inadequate to our needs, our shipping tonnage was allowed to fall to a dangerous level before the proper remedies were applied. The result was that in both wars our greatest danger of failure came in that very element in which we can never afford to take risks—the sea.

RELATIONS WITH COMMANDERS-IN-CHIEF

In the actual theatres of war the general principle is that, having selected the best men available as Commanders-in-Chief, the Government should give them a free hand and back them up to the hilt with a minimum of interference. That principle should rarely be departed from.

There are occasions, however, when the statesmen are bound to step in. If, for example, the strategy of a Commander-in-Chief involves such a drain on the total resources of the State, Empire or Alliance as to imperil the staying power of the nations concerned, or the conduct of some equally essential operation elsewhere, the Governments concerned may have to intervene.

That was the basis of the difficulties that arose in 1917–18 between Mr Lloyd George and his Generals. After the most exhaustive examination he and some of his colleagues were unconvinced by Generals Haig and Robertson that the Flanders operation offered a reasonable prospect of success, and they apprehended that the result must bleed the man-power of the nation white before the United States of America could bring their strength to bear on a sufficient scale to redress the balance. They put up counter-proposals for examination by the General Staff and the High Command in the field. But these were rejected for technical reasons that they could not over-rule, and they realised that, as a matter of principle, it is inadvisable to order Generals to undertake operations in which they do not believe— another of Hitler's worst mistakes, by the way. Somewhat reluctantly, then, they had to give way. As Mr Lloyd George says in his summing-up of this episode—'The fighting of a battle is mainly a decision for the Generals.' * In the result, the Flanders operations followed the course that Mr Lloyd George had predicted; the man-power of the country was reduced so gravely that in the early months of 1918 the essential needs of the ship-building necessary to bring American forces and of other supply and transport services for maintaining the war effort could only be met at the expense of the Army. There followed the grave reverses of March 1918.

The merits of that controversy will not be argued here, because it is a very complicated matter and there is much to be said on both sides. It is only mentioned to illustrate the difficulties in allotting the national resources that may confront Governments, especially in the later stages of a war.

Another reason which may compel intervention by Governments in plans or operations is in the event of a difference of opinion either between the three Fighting Services, or, as more often happens, between the military authorities of the different nations forming an Alliance.

In the last war, for example, there were serious differences of opinion between the British and French military authorities on

* *War Memoirs*, vol. VI, p. 3416.

such matters as the extent of the line to be held by the British Army in France; the maintenance of armies in the Balkans and other so-called 'side-shows'; the command and distribution of naval forces in the Mediterranean (1918); and the establishment of an independent Air Force in 1918. The only way to settle these matters was for the heads of the two Governments to step in.

GERMAN EXPERIENCE

It used to be argued early in the last war that the successes of the Central Powers in the first four years were due to the ascendancy of the military authorities in Germany.

Theoretically the last word rested with the Kaiser, who however seems usually to have given his decision in favour of his military advisers when there was a clash between them and the civilian Ministers—as in the case of the submarine war on shipping. It is clear, however, from the Memoirs of the German leaders that the military authorities did not actually control the civil Government. Ludendorff is always inveighing against the fact that he could not do so, and complained bitterly of the friction that arose in consequence. For example:

G.H.Q. and the Chancellor had equal status. Here, too, the common head was the Emperor. Our dealings with the Imperial Government were frequent, and not too pleasant. We did not meet with that spirit of accommodation which was so necessary when we told the Government what the successful prosecution of the war demanded of them, if the German people were to be rendered capable of victory.

The representation of military interests in all questions of foreign policy during the war and in connection with the conclusion of peace meant frequent dealings, and much friction also.

The machinery of Government in Berlin gave the impression of being extremely clumsy.

The various departments worked side by side without any real sympathy or cohesion, and there was infinite 'over-lapping'. The left hand often did not know what the right was doing. A Bismarck could have made these departments co-operate properly, but the task was beyond our War Chancellors.*

* Ludendorff, *My War Memories*, vol. I, p. 263.

In another passage Ludendorff goes on to compare the German system unfavourably with the British:

> Like Clemenceau and Lloyd George I had wanted to call on the whole nation, but I was not a dictator, as men were only too glad to repeat, false though it was. Lloyd George and Clemenceau had the control of their Parliaments, for these were 'their' Parliaments. At the same time, they stood at the heads of the entire administrative and executive authorities; I, on the other hand, had no constitutional power to influence the German Government in order to enforce my views as to the steps necessary for the conduct of the war, and I was frequently confronted with the lack of understanding and energy of the departments concerned.*

Prince Max of Baden, writing from the civilian side, is no less critical of the German system:

> But Particularism lurks like an inborn curse in the German character, and before the war—and above all, during the war—had taken refuge in the Departments—among the Admirals, among the Generals, among the diplomats. They had no spirit of mutual trust, and seldom worked together as allies in a common cause, as the welfare of the nation required of them.†

From this and other testimony by our enemy we may conclude that the German system was nothing to boast about. Indeed, between the two wars I had it direct more than once from German officials that it was unsatisfactory both in peace and war. When they asked me how team-work and loyalty between Ministers, Military Staffs and Civil Servants had been accomplished in this country, I replied by telling the old story of the American visitor to Cambridge, who asked the gardener of one of the Colleges how the flawless grass in the Court had been achieved, and received the reply: 'By mowin' and rollin' and rollin' and mowin' for about three hundred years.' It was by some such process that our system of Cabinet Government had been evolved, I added—an answer which was considered discouraging!

* Ludendorff, *My War Memories,* vol. II, pp. 706–7.
† *The Memoirs of Prince Max of Baden,* vol. II, p. 285.

For the above reasons we can, I think, accept the proposition that under modern conditions the War Control must rest in the hands of statesmen, working, of course, in the closest co-operation with the Service Chiefs.

THE PRIME MINISTER'S RESPONSIBILITY

The Prime Minister must play the leading part. As the late Lord Morley (then Mr Morley) puts it in his *Life of Walpole*:

The Prime Minister is the keystone of the Cabinet arch. Although in Cabinet all its members stand on an equal footing, speak with equal voice, and, on the rare occasions when a division is taken, are counted on the fraternal system of one man, one vote, yet the head of the Cabinet is *primus inter pares*, and occupies a position which, so long as it lasts, is one of exceptional and peculiar authority.*

In fact John Morley went further and claimed that

The flexibility of the Cabinet system allows the Prime Minister in an emergency to take upon himself a power not inferior to that of a dictator, provided always that the House of Commons will stand by him.†

The truth of that statement is illustrated by the paramount position established by Mr Lloyd George in the last war and by Mr Churchill in the present war.

To tell the truth, though, the job is no bed of roses. 'No English Minister can ever wish for war', says Lord Rosebery in his *Life of Pitt*:

He can reap little glory from success; he is the first scapegoat of failure. He too has to face, not the heroic excitement of the field, but domestic misery and discontent; the heavy burden of taxation, and the unpopularity of the sacrifice which all war entails.‡

Lord Rosebery also warns the war-time Prime Minister against 'that strange bias which has made some eminent statesmen believe themselves to be eminent generals', from which he exonerates Mr Pitt, adding, however, that 'he had the consciousness of a boundless capacity for meeting the real requirements of the

---

* Chapter VII, p. 157.   † *Ibid.* p. 158.   ‡ *Ibid.* p. 117.

country'. I believe consciousness of capacity, rather than personal ambition, is often the real underlying motive which has usually thrown up the right man to lead the Government Control in our great war emergencies.

Apart from his being the 'keystone of the Cabinet arch', there are other reasons why the Prime Minister of the day must be the head of the Government Control. One of the principal responsibilities of the office in peace or war is to expound the main policy of the Government to Parliament, and through Parliament and otherwise—for example, by the broadcast—to the people. In a major war the main policy of the Government is necessarily its conduct. To expound it the Prime Minister must be intimately conversant with all its aspects. The threads must all be in his hands, and that can never be the case unless he is responsible for the day-to-day running of the war. It is not necessary, of course, that the Prime Minister should be burdened with all statements on behalf of the Government, and in December 1916, Mr Lloyd George established a wise precedent, which Mr Churchill has followed in the present war, of delegating the day-to-day leadership of the House of Commons to a colleague.

Another reason is that, from the nature of his office, the Prime Minister has a prestige unequalled among Ministers. Disputes between Departments and their Ministerial Heads are bound to arise, and quite legitimately—for example, on questions of priority, especially in the later stages of a war when resources are strained. Although there are many disputes in which the decision of an unbiased colleague will be accepted by the parties, others arise of such importance that only the Prime Minister's decision will be final. He alone 'carries the guns', and even he will not be able to give right decisions unless he has all the threads of war policy in his hands.

It will be remembered that during the Cabinet crisis of December 1916, which centred in the system of Government Control, Mr Lloyd George proposed that there should be a small War Committee under his own chairmanship which, subject to the authority of the Prime Minister and his discretion to refer any matter to the Cabinet, should undertake the day-to-day direction of the war. That scheme broke down owing to Mr Asquith's insistence that

whatever changes are made in the composition or functions of the War Committee, the Prime Minister must be its Chairman. He cannot be relegated to the position of an arbiter in the background or a referee to the Cabinet. *

The system that Mr Asquith rejected had been tried in the Newcastle-Pitt administration of 1757, of which it was said that 'Mr Pitt *does* everything, and the Duke of Newcastle *gives* everything'. Although, so far as the Seven Years' War was concerned, that experiment, in spite of some failures, produced great results, it is very understandable that Mr Asquith was unwilling to play the part of Newcastle to Mr Lloyd George's Pitt.

All the evidence therefore points to one conclusion, namely, that the Prime Minister, and the Prime Minister alone, must be the head of the Government Control in time of war.

THE PRIME MINISTER AND WAR PREPARATION

Our Prime Ministers, who have had to force their way to the top through the hurly-burly of political life, have nearly always been men of strong character and adaptability to handle crises of every sort and kind. But until the present century at any rate they have rarely had the opportunity to study the problems of wars with which they may be confronted, and that may have some bearing on the fact that our preparations have never been adequate to the emergency when it arose.

Our foreign policy is always and necessarily one of peace, since to a country dependent for its existence on imports of food and raw material, which have to be paid for by exports and invisible exports, peace is the first essential.

* J. A. Spender and Cyril Asquith, *Life of Lord Oxford and Asquith,* vol. II, chapter L, pp. 252–3.

For centuries there was a tendency to trust to principles of peace, of neutrality and of diplomacy as a substitute for war preparation. The risk that war may break out for reasons beyond our control and that our existence may be put in jeopardy has only too often been overlooked.

Thus we see the younger Pitt, bent on a policy of peace, prosperity and reform, ignoring the French Revolution up to the last moment and declaring in February 1792, just a year before the outbreak of the long war of the French Revolution and Empire, that

Unquestionably there never was a time in the history of this country when from the situation of Europe we might more reasonably expect fifteen years of peace than at the present moment.*

And again, more than a century later, we see successive British Governments of different parties adopting an equally complaisant attitude, assuming no major war for ten years† and 'taking risks for peace' up to 1935.‡

How are we to provide against a repetition of those risks? How are we to ensure that in peaceful years a succession of Prime Ministers and other Ministers are sufficiently versed in the business of warfare to be ready to take charge of its direction at short notice? How are we to avoid again being caught napping?

That subject is discussed further in a later chapter, but one essential principle can be stated here and now, namely, that the Prime Minister should always be responsible for the general direction of our preparations for war.

In a sentence, the same considerations which compel the Prime Minister of the day to take charge of the control and direction of war must apply in peace to preparation for war. In addition, what applies to the Prime Minister, on whom so great a burden may suddenly fall in the event of war, must apply to his principal

* Rosebery, *Pitt*, chapter VII, p. 121.
† House of Lords debates, e.g. 7th March 1935.
‡ White Paper on Defence, March 1935. Cmd. 4827/35.

colleagues, who will have to share that burden and one or more of whom may eventually be destined to take his place.

That principle, however, does not provide a panacea, as is shown by the inadequacy of our forces on the outbreak of war in 1914 and again in 1939, when the preparations were supervised by the Prime Ministers of the day. But in both instances our preparations were a great improvement on those made before previous wars, and our forces were just sufficient to avert early disaster and to provide a screen under which we could build up our strength.

CHAPTER II

PREPARATION BEFORE 1914

OUR system of control of preparation for war has for forty years been vested in the Committee of Imperial Defence, with which I was associated from 1908 to 1938.

THE COMMITTEE OF IMPERIAL DEFENCE

So much has been said and written about that institution that it is hardly necessary to describe its history in detail, but, as our own system of Government Control throughout two major wars has been evolved from this Committee, the salient features must be mentioned.

In January 1904 the late Lord Esher's War Office (Reconstitution) Committee, which had been set up as the result of the national heart-burnings over the South African War, issued its first Report, a prescient document devoted exclusively to the Committee of Imperial Defence.

'The British Empire', the Report states, 'is pre-eminently a great Naval, Indian and Colonial Power. There are, nevertheless, no means for co-ordinating defence problems, for dealing with them as a whole, for defining the proper functions of the various elements, and for ensuring that, on the one hand, peace preparations are carried out upon a consistent plan, and on the other hand, that, in time of emergency, a definite war policy, based upon solid data, can be formulated.'

The remedy proposed was a fresh reorganisation of a Cabinet Committee that had been established by the late Lord Salisbury in 1895, and already reorganised once by Mr Balfour after he became Prime Minister in July 1902, with the title of Committee of Imperial Defence. The Esher Committee insisted that the Prime Minister must be its invariable President, and have 'absolute discretion in the selection and variation of its members'. The

Committee was to be advisory and consultative. As the corner-stone of the whole edifice there was to be a small Permanent Secretariat. Mr Balfour at once adopted this proposal, and the Committee of Imperial Defence was brought into existence by a Treasury Minute dated the 4th May 1904.

From that day to this the Committee of Imperial Defence has been the main instrument of Government Control both of pre-paration for war in time of peace, and of Higher Control in time of war, although in the latter case under a different title and with suitable adjustments.

Preparation for war before 1914 can be best examined under the heads of Principles, Policy, Plans and Preparations. These phases tended, of course, to merge into one another—especially the two latter—but nevertheless form convenient subheads.

THE PHASE OF PRINCIPLE*

The Committee of Imperial Defence came into existence when the Anglo-French Entente was taking shape, but before the German menace had come above the horizon. Mr Balfour, the Prime Minister, was assiduous in his attention to the Committee. During his last two years of office he did not miss one of its sixty meetings. Its early years were devoted largely to the formulation of principles to govern our defence policy. The vital importance of sea power as the basis of Imperial Defence came to the fore-front with a drastic reorganisation of the fleet under Lord Fisher. Principles were established to govern the scale of our coast defences at home and abroad, and the size of their garrisons, which were being overhauled. Meanwhile the War Office was busy applying the later recommendations of the Esher Com-mittee, from which further principles emerged. The phase of principle provided solid foundations on which to build.

* Based on the author's lecture at London University, 12th March 1927, published afterwards in *The Army Quarterly*.

THE PHASE OF POLICY*

The phase of policy began in 1907 with an inquiry by a Sub-Committee under Mr Morley, then Secretary of State for India, into the Defence of India. It is necessary to recall this because the needs of India provided, rather oddly, the governing factor in the size of the Army.

But about the time of the change of Government in December 1905, the attitude of Germany was causing disquiet. A year or two later Field-Marshal Lord Roberts wrote to Sir Henry Campbell-Bannerman calling attention to the dangers of invasion. Early in 1908 a Sub-Committee was set up under Mr Asquith, the Chancellor of the Exchequer, who shortly after became Prime Minister, but continued his investigation of this problem.

That was the real starting point of our defensive preparations against aggression by Germany. The decision went against Lord Roberts, and the governing conclusions were:

1. That so long as our naval supremacy is assured against any reasonably probable combination of Powers, invasion is impracticable.
2. That if we permanently lose command of the sea, whatever may be the strength and organisation of the home force, the subjection of the country to the enemy is inevitable.
3. That our army for home defence ought to be sufficient in number and organisation not only to repel small raids, but to compel an enemy who contemplates invasion to come with so substantial a force as will make it impossible for him to evade our fleets.
4. That to ensure an ample margin of safety such a force may, for purposes of calculation, be assumed to be 70,000 men.†

....

That exhaustive inquiry could not take place without raising the position of France, our potential Ally, and Belgium. On the day following the completion of the Invasion Inquiry, therefore, Mr Asquith appointed a fresh Sub-Committee of the Committee

* Based on the author's lecture at London University; Lord Oxford and Asquith, *The Genesis of the War*; Winston Churchill, *World Crisis*; Callwell, *Field-Marshal Sir Henry Wilson*.
† *The Genesis of the War*, p. 115.

of Imperial Defence, at which he himself again presided, to inquire into the military needs of the Empire—excluding India and Egypt, both of which were now being dealt with by Sub-Committees under Mr Morley.

The new inquiry brought the Sub-Committee into the very heart of a Continental war—what was to be done if France was attacked; the Belgian Treaty of 1839, guaranteeing the independence of Belgium—the famous 'scrap of paper'; the problems of Holland, Denmark, etc.

There was at that time a cleavage of opinion between the heads of the Admiralty and War Office as to whether the Expeditionary Force ought, in the event of war with Germany, to be committed at the outset to go to the aid of France. The General Staff urged it strongly, and, it will be remembered, had been allowed to hold conversations with the French General Staff as to how we could best help, but without accepting any commitment. But the Admiralty held the view, which they did not abandon until after the Agadir crisis of 1911, that our Army might be required elsewhere; that it was too small to make the difference between success and failure on the Continent, and should not be irretrievably committed at the outset of a war. They attached great importance also to economic pressure based on naval action.

The net result of the inquiry was that the General Staff was allowed to work out its plans on the assumption that an expeditionary force might be sent to the Continent, but the decision was left for the Government of the day if and when the occasion arose.

In the year 1909 a long inquiry took place, again under Mr Asquith's chairmanship, into the naval policy and plans for war, in which Lord Charles Beresford and Admiral Custance took Lord Roberts' place as *advocati diaboli*. Every aspect was probed, and the result was to put the Admiralty on their mettle with a general tuning up of the whole machine, including the first steps towards the creation of the great Naval Staff that in later years has played so important a part. The Report was published as a White Paper.

The late Lord Oxford, therefore, was justified when he wrote:

It would not be an unjust claim to say that the Government had by that date [August 1909] investigated the whole of the ground covered by a possible war with Germany—the naval position; the possibilities of blockade; the invasion problem; the Continental problem; the Egyptian problem. *

And he might have added 'the Defence of India'.

THE PHASE OF PLANS AND PREPARATIONS†

Planning was at once put in hand by the Admiralty and War Office to implement the various decisions on policy, and their plans were supplemented by concerted preparations by other Government Departments and national bodies on such subjects as what was to be done with enemy and neutral merchant ships, their crews and cargoes in the ports of the Empire or captured and brought into port on the outbreak of war—a matter that was complicated by a rather obscure Hague Treaty; trading with the enemy, including besides direct trade, banking, insurance, trade through neutrals; our own supplies; trade protection, which raised the large question of the war insurance of ships and cargoes; the control of railways and ports; censorship in all its branches; protection of vulnerable points; arrangements with the press; treatment of aliens; measures to counter German espionage; cable and wireless communications, including an order of priority for the thousands of messages to be sent by cable and telegraph on the outbreak of war, so as to avoid congesting the lines, and the cutting of the enemy's cables.

These, and many other matters, were dealt with by the Committee of Imperial Defence, working through Sub-Committees, which reported to the parent body under Mr Asquith's invariable chairmanship. Among the steps taken under this procedure was the foundation of the Royal Flying Corps with a Naval Wing and a Military Wing. This was the ancestor of the Royal Air Force and came into existence in 1912, after a false start in 1909.

* *The Genesis of the War*, chapter xv, p. 116.
† *The Genesis of the War. Official History. Naval Operations* (Corbett, J. S.), vol. I, chapter I; *Official History. Seaborne Trade* (Fayle), vol. I.

When completed the plans and preparations were not just pigeon-holed and forgotten. They were handed over to an organisation known as the Co-ordination Committee, and incorporated in a document known as the War Book, in which the responsibility of every Government Department under every heading of war emergency action was laid down both for a Precautionary Stage and a War Stage. It was designed to show every Department, not only what it had to do itself, but what other Departments were doing in the matter. Every piece of legislation; every set of instructions; every order, letter, cable, telegram, including those to fleets, military stations, the Dominions, India and the Colonies (some taking the form of dormant instructions in their possession) was drafted and kept ready for issue.

All necessary papers, orders in council and proclamations were printed or set up in type, and so far was the system carried that the King never moved without having with him those which required his immediate signature. *

The whole was kept continuously up to date by a small standing body to meet the changes and additions required from time to time.

All these matters had to be worked out by the exercise of forethought and imagination, for we had had no experience of a major war for nearly a century.

EMPIRE CO-OPERATION†

Large measures of co-operation between the naval and military forces of the Empire in such matters as similar armaments, textbooks, manuals of instruction and exchanges of Staff Officers were concerted at Imperial Conferences in 1907 and 1909. During the Conference of 1911 the Prime Ministers of the Dominions came to the Committee of Imperial Defence to hear and discuss

---

* *Official History. Naval Operations* (Corbett, J. S.), vol. I, chapter I, p. 20. Longmans, Green & Co.
† Author's lecture to London University, and his article in *The Nineteenth Century and After*, July 1943.

an illuminating and prophetic statement by Sir Edward Grey, which has since been published in the Gooch-Temperley papers on the Origins of the War. In 1912 Sir Robert Borden came to London and heard similar statements, and thereafter other representatives of the Dominions attended the Committee of Imperial Defence from time to time, including Sir George Perley, who arrived in 1914 to represent Canada permanently on the Committee. In all the Dominions defence preparations were made before the war to correspond, *mutatis mutandis*, with our own.

POSITION IN 1914

Sir Julian Corbett summed up the position very fairly in the *Official History. Naval Operations* as follows:

Amongst the many false impressions that prevailed, when after the lapse of a century we found ourselves involved in a great war, not the least erroneous is the belief that we were not prepared for it. Whether the scale on which we prepared was as large as the signs of the times called for, whether we did right to cling to our long-tried system of a small Army and a large Navy, are questions that will long be debated; but, given the scale which we deliberately chose to adopt, there is no doubt that the machinery for setting our forces in action had reached an ordered completeness in detail that has no parallel in our history. [*]

Brigadier-General Sir James Edmonds, the distinguished author of the *Official History. Military Operations*, and an outspoken critic on occasions, also states:

Altogether, Britain never yet entered upon any war with anything approaching such forwardness and forethought in the preparation of the scanty military resources at the disposal of the War Office.[†]

Those extracts bring out not only our strength, but the main weakness, namely, that our Army was much too small. In addition we had no scheme prepared beforehand for its rapid expansion, and for the proper ordering of our man-power or for the mobilisation of industry. How did this come about?

[*] Sir Julian S. Corbett, *Official History. Naval Operations*, vol. I, chapter I, p. 18.
[†] Sir James Edmonds, *Official History. Military Operations, France and Belgium*, vol. I, Introduction, p. 13.

REASON FOR SMALL ARMY

For the root cause we should have to go back to the long tradition against the maintenance of a large standing army, which grew up after Cromwell's Protectorate and was revived by James II's attempt to use the army to uproot the protestant religion, as described by the Master of Trinity in his *History of England.* * Tradition, which lingered long, combined with economy, confidence in the protection of the Navy, a belief that armies are an instrument of aggression, and perhaps an instinctive dislike of 'foot slogging', to keep the British army small. At the outset of the War of the Spanish Succession the number of soldiers to be supplied by England was voted by Parliament at the figure of 40,000, but only 18,000 were to be British and the remainder foreigners in British pay. Even the 18,000 had to be raised on the basis of a standing army of 7,000, the figure to which it had been cut down four years earlier by the Treaty of Ryswick. In the Peninsular War (1808–1814) the strength of the British army never exceeded 30,000 British at a time. At the outset of the Crimean War, according to Oman, we were

utterly unprepared for war. The army was weak in numbers, and had been woefully neglected for the last forty years.... With some difficulty an expeditionary force of 28,000 men was collected and sent to the East....†

The South African War of 1899–1902 once more revealed serious shortcomings in our Army. After that war the question of Army organisation was taken seriously in hand.

One of the most important results was the crystallisation of the various staff elements already existing into a General Staff, to which Mr Haldane gave the finishing touches.

But all Haldane's work, admirable as it was, did not produce when war broke out an Army adequate to our needs or an organisation to expand it. It seems curious, in retrospect, that the

* Book IV, chapters VI and VII.
† Oman, *History of England*, chapter XLI, p. 684.

various inquiries on policy already referred to did not bring out these needs. But, as already mentioned, Lord Roberts' case for an army for Home Defence did not succeed and he did not follow it up into the wider issues. Neither did the inquiry into the Continental problem show that, on a comparison of the French and Russian strength with that of Germany, a larger British army was essential. We over-rated the efficiency of our potential Allies, and under-rated that of Germany. So the expeditionary force remained at the figure resulting from the inquiry into the Defence of India—six divisions.

There were, of course, great difficulties in producing a compulsory army side by side with the voluntary army required for Empire Defence, and politically, apart from the traditional British dislike of large armies, which was perhaps over-rated, compulsory service was not popular among the masses. As Mr Asquith put it:

Any Government which proposed it would have committed political suicide. It would have split the Cabinet, split the House of Commons, split both political parties, and split the whole nation;...*

TRADITIONAL PEACE POLICY

It cannot be emphasised too strongly also that the Liberal Government of that day was following the traditional policy of peace, which has already been touched on. The result was that all our policy of war preparation was of a defensive character and essentially unprovocative. Compulsory military service was considered as likely to precipitate the very catastrophe that we were striving by might and main to avert by our peace policy. That policy also accounted for the handicap to the free exercise of sea power, which was accepted in the Declaration of London and other international treaties and bore heavily on us in the early part of the war.

* *The Genesis of the War*, pp. 138 and 139.

The basis, then, of all our preparations conformed fairly closely to the following principle laid down in Hobbes' *Leviathan* in 1651:

> And consequently it is a precept, or generall rule of Reason, *That every man, ought to endeavour Peace, as farre as he has hope of obtaining it; and when he cannot obtain it, that he may seek, and use, all helps, and advantages of Warre.* The first branch of which Rule, containeth the first, and Fundamentall Law of Nature; which is *to seek Peace, and follow it.* The Second, the summe of the Right of Nature; which is, *By all means we can to defend our selves.* *

CONCLUSION

Whether that principle was sound or not, whether, in fact, it corresponded to the prevailing national sentiment or not, this much can be said in its favour, that within a narrow interpretation of a defensive policy our war preparations were successful. No invasion took place. British territory all over the world remained substantially intact. Sea communications were maintained, even though with grievous losses from U-boat attack later in the war. And under this secure shield of sea power we were able to organise the vast resources by which, in co-operation with our Allies, we achieved victory. But without a doubt we took risks.

* Part I, chapter xiv.

CHAPTER III

THE GREAT WAR 1914–18

CICERO laid down that 'armies can signify but little abroad, unless there be counsel and wise management at home'.* In this chapter the development of 'counsel and wise management' during the Great War of 1914–18 will be traced at home, in the Empire, and among the Allies as a whole.

GOVERNMENT CONTROL AT HOME†

In discussing the defects in our war preparations in the first chapter, one was deliberately omitted, as it seemed more appropriate to the second—namely, the absence of any pre-war plans for the reorganisation of the Government for control in war.

My own idea was that the Committee of Imperial Defence should be reorganised and tuned up to the pitch of actual war and should take over the control. That is what eventually happened, but it took longer than was expected, and nearly two and a half years of trial and error elapsed before a really satisfactory system was evolved.

When war broke out Mr Asquith carried on with the former Cabinet, from which Lord Morley and Mr John Burns had resigned. During the days of crisis the full Cabinet had been in constant session and it remained so for three or four months after the declaration of war. The only deliberate devolution of Cabinet authority, and that a temporary one, was on August 5th, the day following the outbreak of war, when Mr Asquith summoned Lord Haldane, Sir Edward Grey, Mr Churchill, the First Sea

---

* Cicero, *The Offices*, Book I, chapter 22.
† Among many authorities are: The *Official Histories*. Lord Oxford, *The Genesis of the War*. The First Report of the Dardanelles Commission. The author's lecture at London University, 11th March 1927. Sir William Robertson, *Soldiers and Statesmen*. Winston Churchill, *The World Crisis*. Callwell, *Field-Marshal Sir Henry Wilson*. David Lloyd George, *War Memoirs*. The War Cabinet Report for 1917.

Lord, Field-Marshals Lord Roberts and Lord Kitchener,* and all the leading Generals to a Council of War (not to be confused with the later War Council) to consider what number of troops should be sent to the Continent and where they should be concentrated. After two meetings the conclusion was reached in effect that the War Office should send four of the available six divisions and a cavalry division to France, the other two divisions following as soon as they could be spared from Home Defence. The preconcerted plans for the transport and concentration of the force were carried out with complete smoothness and almost uncanny secrecy.

These two meetings encouraged the hope that the nucleus of Ministers present at the Council of War would become a standing War Council for the day-to-day control of the war. The time however had not come for that. The Higher Control remained firmly vested in the Cabinet of twenty-one members. Meanwhile the Committee of Imperial Defence and its Sub-Committees were used mainly for dealing with questions of Home Defence, except for one Sub-Committee which started on the first day of the war to plan the various minor expeditions against the German Colonies and did some admirable work.

This system continued for nearly four months, but proved unsatisfactory. The Cabinet was too large to meet day in and day out, and too cumbrous to be called together rapidly at short notice.† It did not work to an Agenda Paper and had no Secretary and no records. Ministers sometimes misapprehended the decisions, and the Staffs of the Admiralty and War Office and the Civil Service Chiefs were often in the dark as to what had been decided and what action they had to take. One might compare it to Bacon's account of the councils of his time:

> The counsels at this day in most places are but familiar meetings where matters are rather talked on than debated. And they run too swift to the order or act of counsel.   (*Of Counsel.*)

* By the time of the second meeting on 6th August Lord Kitchener had become Secretary of State for War.
† First Report of Dardanelles Commission.

To add to the confusion a practice grew up, as several of the Memoirs record, of meetings of little groups of Ministers at odd hours, perhaps late at night, to deal with some unexpected emergency. Again there was no Secretary, no record. The decisions may have been reported briefly at the next meeting of the Cabinet, but in the welter of business, Ministers with their own claims to press were apt to overlook them. It was hard to find out what was afoot, and consequently to secure co-ordination, in which Mr Asquith had asked my help. This tendency towards an unofficial Inner Cabinet was unpopular and suspect, as such manifestations usually are, tending to weaken the team-work of the Government as a whole.

For long-range planning the Cabinet was utterly unsuited. That did not matter much while the pre-war plans were working themselves out. But in October 1914, when war threatened with Turkey, further planning was essential, and, outside of the Admiralty and War Office, this system made no provision for it. Moreover, by this time the strain on Ministers of continuous Cabinet meetings, superimposed on their Parliamentary duties, and the novel and heavy administrative effort that war had placed on their Departments, was beginning to tell.

SECRECY

Secrecy, too, so vitally important in planning, was not facilitated by a large Cabinet. Listen for a moment to what the ancients have to say about secrecy.

Polybius, for example, in discussing the Art of Commanding Armies, says:

Now the head and front of such precautions is silence; and not to allow either joy at the appearance of an unexpected hope, or fear, or familiarity, or natural affection, to induce a man to communicate his plans to any one unconcerned, but to impart it to those and those alone without whom it is impossible to complete his plan; and not even to them a moment sooner than necessary, but only when the exigencies of the particular service make it inevitable. It is necessary, moreover, not only to be silent with the tongue, but much more so in the mind....

(*The Histories of Polybius*, Book IX, chapter XIII.)

Thomas à Kempis wisely writes:

Often times I could wish that I had held my peace when I have spoken; and that I had not been in company.

And again:

The most part of men are given to talk much, and therefore little confidence is to be placed in them.   (*Of the Imitation of Christ.*)

Thomas Carlyle says the same thing in characteristic language:

For men are very porous; weighty secrets oozing out of them, like quicksilver through clay jars.

(*Frederick the Great*, Book XVI, chapter VII.)

Bacon suggests—not without some justification—that leakage often comes from the top:

But let princes beware that the unsecreting of their affairs comes not from themselves. And as for Cabinet counsels, it may be their motto, '*Plenus rimarum sum*' (I am full of leaks): one futile person, that maketh it his glory to tell, will do more hurt than many, that know it their duty to conceal.   (*Of Counsel.*)

And, in the following, he must surely have had a vision of enquiries to which Ministers are often exposed in the Lobbies:

They will so beset a man with questions, and draw him on, and pick it out of him, that, without an absurd silence, he must show an inclination one way: or, if he do not, they will gather as much by his silence as by his speech.   (*Of Simulation and Dissimulation.*)

All this would have appealed very strongly to Lord Kitchener, who was always very secretive with his colleagues.

Thomas Hobbes provides the antidote to these dangers:

Fourthly, in deliberations that ought to be kept secret (whereof there be many occasions in Publique Businesse), the Counsells of many, and especially in Assemblies, are dangerous; And therefore great Assemblies are necessitated to commit such affaires to lesser numbers, and of such persons as are most versed, and in whose fidelity they have most confidence.   (*Leviathan*, Part 2, chapter XXV.)

THE WAR COUNCIL

And that is exactly what Mr Asquith did. At the end of November 1914, he set up a War Council, committing part at any rate of the Government Control to lesser numbers. Originally it was composed of eight persons, including the two Chiefs of Staff: Mr Asquith, Mr Lloyd George, Sir Edward Grey, Mr Churchill and Lord Fisher his new First Sea Lord, Lord Kitchener and his new Chief of the Imperial General Staff, General Sir James Wolfe Murray, and Mr Balfour, with myself as Secretary.

The War Council was an adaptation of the Committee of Imperial Defence to war conditions. The nucleus of key members was the same. The inclusion of Mr Balfour, who sat in Parliament on the front Opposition Bench, was not unprecedented in the procedure of the Committee. He had been consulted by the Invasion Committee of 1907-8, and had been a member of a Sub-Committee that overhauled the same subject in 1913-14.

The procedure of the War Council was the same as that of the Committee of Imperial Defence, except that the Council did not work to an Agenda Paper, and for reasons of secrecy I kept the Minutes in manuscript—a most laborious job in the stress of war.

The Council did not meet continuously to deal with the day-to-day business of Government Control, but, to use Mr Asquith's own language, was only summoned 'when serious questions involving new departures in policy or joint strategic operations arose'.* And it came to pass that the main new departure and the principal joint strategic operations for which the War Council made itself responsible were the Dardanelles attacks divided into two parts—the naval attacks from mid-February to mid-March 1915, and, after their failure, the landings on the Gallipoli Peninsula begun on 25th April.

These operations were too long for description in detail here, but a few of the defects in the region of Government Control,

* *Memories and Reflections*, vol. II, chapter VIII, p. 87.

emerging from the numerous published accounts,* which contributed to failure deserve mention:

(i) The Staff Organisation was defective. The Admiralty and War Office Staffs were not in close and daily contact, like the three Service Staffs in the present War Cabinet organisation. The Admiralty War Staff, as it was called, was comparatively new and had not yet reached its final form. The First Sea Lord was half-hearted about the naval attempt to force the Dardanelles. The War Office General Staff and its Chief were completely dominated by the overwhelming personality of Lord Kitchener. Its principal officers had gone to France with the Expeditionary Force and had been replaced by retired officers on the Reserve List, including some good men, but without the prestige and close unity of their predecessors.

(ii) There was no machinery for Joint Planning, which militated gravely against the success of the joint campaign. The result was that the planning for the Dardanelles was too much departmentalised. Insufficient examination was given to the question of the drain that would be made on our war effort in the event of military operations being undertaken. The War Council did not insist on being furnished with joint appreciations by the two Staffs.

(iii) The method under which the Council met, only when new departures were involved, was insufficient. The day-to-day situation was such that it ought to have been kept under continuous observation, either by the War Council itself or by some smaller body appointed by it.

The fact is that we were still groping our way towards a better system. The War Council was an improvement on the earlier plan of Control by a large Cabinet, but was very far from meeting the needs of Government Control in War.

THE DARDANELLES COMMITTEE

On the fall of the Liberal Government, owing partly to the failures at the Dardanelles, and partly to the munitions scandal, but actually precipitated by Lord Fisher's resignation, Mr Asquith's Coalition Government adopted a new system, under which the

---

* *First Report of Dardanelles Commission. Official History. Military Operations. Gallipoli* (Aspinall-Oglander), vol. I, chapter IV. Robertson, *Soldiers and Statesmen.* Winston Churchill, *The World Crisis.*

Cabinet retained control, but delegated the supervision of the Dardanelles operations to a Cabinet Committee known as the Dardanelles Committee. I was again Secretary.

That, as Lord Kitchener was swift to see, was an unworkable plan. The war could not be dealt with in compartments. The various fronts were inseparable. Naval reinforcements for the Dardanelles could only be sent at the expense of either the fleets at sea or trade protection; military reinforcements and war material, which was in very short supply, only at the cost of the Expeditionary Force in France. Major war is always total and must not be too much sectionalised.

Another defect that soon manifested itself was an increase in the numbers of the Committee. That nearly always happens. In the case of the Committee of Imperial Defence, for example, before 1914 a number of 'Elder Statesmen' had gradually been added—Lord Haldane, Lord Morley, Lord Kitchener, Lord Fisher, Sir Arthur Wilson, Sir John French—after they ceased to hold offices entitling them to membership, so that the Committee had become as unwieldy as the Cabinet itself. Similarly, the War Council had grown from an original 8 to 13 members, and now the Dardanelles Committee from the original over-large 11 members increased to 12, to whom must be added the First Sea Lord and the Chief of the Imperial General Staff who, though not original members, usually attended, making 14 in all.

A third defect was that, as in the case of the War Council, the members were all overburdened with departmental and Parliamentary duties.

In some respects, however, the Dardanelles Committee was an improvement on the War Council. It met more regularly and, in spite of its title, tended, under Mr Asquith's adroit management, more and more to take charge of the day-to-day running of the war as a whole. The Chiefs of Staff also had begun to work better together.

The failure at Suvla Bay, however, brought the Dardanelles Committee into disrepute, and in November 1915, Mr Asquith, partly under Parliamentary pressure, especially from Sir Edward Carson, who had resigned office shortly before, decided on a reorganisation of the system of Government Control. He scrapped the Dardanelles Cabinet Committee and substituted a War Committee. At the first meeting only the Prime Minister, Lord Kitchener and Mr Balfour, the First Lord, were present, without even a Secretary, although I was called in afterwards to record the decisions and thereafter attended regularly as Secretary.

At the next meeting Sir Edward Grey and Mr Lloyd George were added, and Mr McKenna immediately after, and Mr Asquith announced in Parliament on 11th November that there were six members. As time went on the number was raised to eleven, making with the First Sea Lord and Chief of the Imperial General Staff, who were nearly always present and virtually members, thirteen members.

As an organisation, however, the War Committee was a vast improvement on its predecessors. Joint memoranda and appreciations were provided regularly by the General Staffs of the Admiralty and War Office. Sir Archibald Murray and his successor, Sir William Robertson, had built up a reliable General Staff in the War Office. In the Secretariat we had learned a good deal. Team-work was everywhere much improved.

As the war spread over the world, as new theatres of war opened up, the scope of the War Committee inevitably widened. The losses from U-boat warfare, combined with the neglect of shipbuilding in the early years, and the increased demands of the new theatres of war and the growth of our armies, brought shipping to the front, as always, as the key to victory. Great policies were required to compensate for shipping losses; an increase in tonnage, a reduction in imports by stimulating agriculture and all kinds of production, and curtailment of civilian requirements.

These measures could not brook delay, so gradually and inevitably the War Committee spread out its tentacles and grasped these and many other subjects in turn. In the autumn of 1916 the War Committee was fulfilling nearly all the functions of Government Control—in a sort of way.

In a sort of way—yes: but in spite of many improvements the machine was too weak for all these extensions of function. Not only was the War Committee too large, but again there were not enough unencumbered members concentrating on the central problems of the war.

Moreover, as anyone who studies the various Memoirs can see, the Government itself, in spite of the brilliancy of its members, was a coalition of parties that never really coalesced. It was a mechanical mixture, not a chemical compound, a Coalition and not a National Government.

Those were the root causes that brought the Government down in December 1916, though the occasion was controversy within the Cabinet over the structure of the Control of the war.

THE WAR CABINET*

On coming into office on 7th December 1916, Mr Lloyd George at once reorganised the whole system of Government Control in such a way as to remove previous weaknesses.

First he reduced the numbers. The War Cabinet which he founded was composed of only five members—the Prime Minister as Chairman, Mr Bonar Law as Leader of the House of Commons and Chancellor of the Exchequer, Lord Curzon as Lord President of the Council (in those days a light office), Lord Milner and Mr Arthur Henderson, Ministers without Portfolio. The number never exceeded seven.

Next, with the exception of Mr Bonar Law, all the members were free from heavy administrative and Parliamentary duties and able to give their whole time and energy to the central problems of the war. Lord Curzon and the two Ministers without

* The War Cabinet Reports, 1917 and 1918.

Portfolio were able to relieve the Prime Minister and War Cabinet of much detail, and occasionally to undertake missions abroad, such as Lord Milner's mission to Russia in January 1917, Mr Henderson's later and less fortunate mission to that country, and later on General Smuts' numerous travels. It became customary to refer complicated interdepartmental questions involving a lot of detail to one or other of these three Ministers and later to General Smuts also with authority sometimes to investigate and report to the Cabinet, sometimes to settle and administer. This was done *ad hoc*.

The system was essentially flexible, and subjects were redistributed to meet changing circumstances. That method is preferable to any rigid distribution of subjects between members of the War Cabinet, as each interdepartmental issue is usually found to concern a different group of Government Departments. When major issues of policy arose, the subject would be brought back by the member in charge to the War Cabinet, or occasionally, as in the case of the German submarine campaign, the Prime Minister, with the prestige of his office, would take it over for a time.

The War Cabinet therefore became in effect the Supreme Control in commission with the Prime Minister as the dominating and directing force, but it was supplemented by this system of delegation, which provided a safeguard against congestion of business.

Owing to its small numbers, the War Cabinet was able to meet *de die in diem* and at the shortest notice. In 1917 it met more than 300 times.

Though he worked his team very hard, Mr Lloyd George believed in keeping them fit. As he himself was not addicted to late hours, after-dinner meetings were rare, and in the whole period (including the frequent inter-allied Conferences at home and abroad) I have not been able to trace more than half-a-dozen late-night meetings. On one occasion when he found his colleagues showing signs of strain he ordered them into 'rest camp', adjourning the meetings for a few days, though he was unable to take advantage of it himself owing to some domestic crisis. That illustrates one of the first principles in Government Control, namely that for all those who share this great responsibility—the first essential is to keep fit.

The new War Cabinet kept regular Minutes and worked to an Agenda Paper. As Bacon puts it:

It were better that, in causes of weight, the matter were propounded one day and not spoken to till the next day; *in nocte consilium.*

(*Of Counsel.*)

For the first time in history a Secretary attended the meetings to record its proceedings. The Chiefs of Staff were present for the discussion of military questions. Thus the War Cabinet combined in itself the powers of decision of the former Cabinet with the systematic procedure of the Committee of Imperial Defence.

One great advantage of the new method was that divided responsibility was avoided. In the case of the previous organisations the final word had rested with the Cabinet, with the possibility of divided responsibility. It was not often that the Cabinet had intervened except in very important matters, but instances could be mentioned when this had occurred. The most notable was over the evacuation of the Gallipoli Peninsula. On 22nd November 1915 the War Committee had, after exhaustive examination of the whole situation, advised immediate evacuation of the whole Peninsula. The Cabinet then insisted on re-opening the whole question, and did not confirm the War Committee's view until 17th December. The result was that Anzac and Suvla were not evacuated until 20th December (nearly a month after the War Committee's decision), and Cape Helles only on 8th January. Those delays occurred at a time when the weather was liable to break at any moment.*

Although under Providence both evacuations were carried out successfully by General (now Field-Marshal Lord) Birdwood,

* *Official History. Military Operations. Gallipoli*, vol. II, chapters xxx and xxxi.

great risks were undoubtedly run by the delay, and the episode well illustrates the danger of divided responsibility in Government Control.

In the new organisation elaborate arrangements were made to keep Ministers outside the War Cabinet (who included all the Secretaries of State) informed on the proceedings of the War Cabinet, so as to ensure that Departmental administration conformed to policy.

Mr Balfour, Secretary of State for Foreign Affairs, was placed in an especially favourable position, and was allowed to attend whenever he chose.

To him, to the other Secretaries of State, and to a number of other principal Departmental Ministers, were sent the documentation of the War Cabinet. Weekly Reports, some prepared in the Secretariat, others in Government Departments, were circulated widely among Ministers.

In addition all Ministers were invited to attend *ad hoc* for the discussions of those items of the Agenda Papers in which their Departments were concerned either directly or indirectly and took a full part in the discussions. Only in the event of an irreconcilable difference of opinion would the War Cabinet, after hearing both sides of the case, meet alone to take a decision.

Another innovation was that Ministers were allowed to bring their principal officials if they desired, and chairmen of committees whose reports were under consideration were usually invited. In the first year of the War Cabinet's existence some 250 persons other than members of the War Cabinet or Secretariat attended meetings.

Copies of the documents prepared for each subject were, of course, sent to all the Ministers concerned in it. In addition, special Reports were prepared in the Secretariat to keep Ministers informed of purely political developments in the eastern and western hemispheres respectively.

Finally, Mr Lloyd George often used to meet his colleagues informally at breakfast, Conservatives one week, Liberal and

Labour the next, to give them an appreciation of the war and of the political situation.

This system of distribution of information did a great deal to avoid the misunderstandings liable to arise in a large Government under a War Cabinet system.

The system involved very heavy work for the Secretariat.

Normally I was allowed the presence of an Assistant-Secretary at the War Cabinet, but I took the numerous ultra-secret meetings single-handed, sometimes keeping the record in manuscript.

Mr Lloyd George left me a free hand in organising the Secretariat, and, a day or two after the Government came into office, I sat up very late one night drafting the scheme in detail, much of which survives to this day in the procedure of the War Cabinet Offices. My assistants were a splendid set of men and soon worked up into a grand team. They included Mr Leo Amery, now Secretary of State for India; Mr Ormsby Gore, now Lord Harlech, until recently British High Commissioner in South Africa; Sir Leslie Wilson, the Governor of Queensland; Major-General Sir Ernest Swinton, famous for his work on tanks; Mr Tom Jones, now Secretary of the Pilgrim Trust; Mr Clement Jones, very well known at Chatham House, who has also worked with me throughout the present war; Mr G. M. Young, and others who have since died.

I cannot pass over the splendid work of my head clerks, my personal staff—including Mr Cyril Longhurst, who had been in the office of the Committee of Imperial Defence since its foundation; Mr Sylvester, afterwards so long associated with Mr Lloyd George; Captain Burgis, my trusted Private Secretary for seventeen years (who is still in the Offices of the War Cabinet), and those responsible for the wonderful indexes that enabled us at a moment's notice to turn up any previous decision required in Cabinet discussion.

Accuracy, speed and secrecy were our aim. I do not believe that any Government office in any country has achieved a higher standard of morale or of rapid and efficient service, and I am proud to record that under Sir Edward Bridges and General Sir Hastings Ismay, the two pillars of the present system, the tradition is maintained at the highest level, under even more difficult circumstances, to this very hour.

Efficiency in war or in any Cabinet business depends on reducing every process to the shortest possible time, on synchronisation, on accuracy, on secrecy, and other details. As Bacon says:

> A long table and a square table, or seats about the walls, seem things of form, but are things of substance; for at a long table a few at the upper end, in effect, sway all the business; but in the other form there is more use of the counsellors' opinions that sit lower.   (*Of Counsel.*)

But the list of important details could be multiplied many times.

THE IMPERIAL WAR CABINET*

The story of Government Control in the Great War would not be complete without some reference to the methods adopted for co-ordinating the effort of the Empire.

Until Mr Lloyd George came into office not much was done beyond the interchange of information and consultation by cable, supplemented by occasional visits to London by individual Prime Ministers, including Sir Robert Borden of Canada, Mr Hughes of Australia, Mr Massey of New Zealand and other Ministers, not simultaneously but at different times. On such occasions the Prime Ministers attended meetings of the War Committee. Low's famous cartoon depicting Mr Asquith's Cabinet cowering under the table before Mr Hughes' thunder, and the Prime Minister calling out 'Tell him in Welsh, George', will long be remembered.

---

* War Cabinet Report, 1917, and *The War Memoirs* of David Lloyd George, chapter LV.

One of the first acts of the new War Cabinet in December 1916 was to invite the Dominions' Prime Ministers and other representatives to an Imperial War Conference during which they would attend a series of special and continuous meetings of the War Cabinet.

These meetings, which began in March 1917, became known as an Imperial War Cabinet—aptly described by Sir Robert Borden as a Cabinet of Nations. In some Dominions the title was not popular and it has not survived, but the foundation was laid of an intimacy in exchange of views which resembled that of a Cabinet, and has continued at Imperial Conferences ever since. I was Secretary of the Imperial War Cabinet and of all subsequent Imperial Conferences held in London until 1938.

At the first session in 1917 much time was devoted to the interchange of full information on all aspects of the war and of policy. But, in addition, reports were prepared by Committees under Lord Curzon and Lord Milner respectively on Territorial and Economic desiderata, which had an important bearing on the policy of the Empire Governments at the Peace Conference.

We sometimes read in the press that the Government were caught napping by the sudden end to the last war with no preparations for peace. As a matter of fact, as shown in Mr Lloyd George's massive *Memoirs*, our war aims were worked out in detail, concerted with both the Empire Prime Ministers and our principal Allies, and announced to the world long before the end of the war.

General Smuts, representing General Botha, played an important part in these discussions and remained in London until the end of the war to assist the War Cabinet.

The second session of the Imperial War Cabinet in June–August 1918 was even more notable. As a result of the first session an improvement had taken place in the quantity and quality of the information sent to the Dominions and India, and, as a result, their representatives came to the Imperial War Cabinet with a much improved background of knowledge, and, to quote

Mr Winston Churchill, 'centred in a single executive the world-spread resources of the British Monarchy'.*

One result of the Imperial War Cabinet was that Mr Lloyd George was able to represent the views of the whole Empire at meetings of the Supreme War Council.

THE SUPREME WAR COUNCIL†

That brings us to War Control among Allies.

In the first few months of the war that object, so far as it was achieved at all, resulted from contacts between Sir John French and General Joffre and occasional visits by individual British or French Ministers to Paris and London respectively.

Lord Kitchener and Lord Esher, who had a post in Paris, early foresaw the need of some closer organisation, but it was not possible to bring it about at first.

Nevertheless, from 5th July 1915 onwards a system of fairly frequent meetings of inter-allied Conferences, at first between the British and French Governments and military authorities only, but later including the Italians and Russians (for which Russian Ministers were rarely forthcoming), grew up and was systematised to a limited extent. I was nearly always British Secretary of these meetings, sometimes in conjunction with a representative of the Foreign Office and/or of the Quai d'Orsay, but sometimes single-handed.

Mr Lloyd George was never satisfied with these arrangements. He felt that the Conferences of Commanders-in-Chief and the Chiefs of Staff, who advised the allied meetings of Ministers, did not get to grips. What he aimed at was some much closer system of planning and control, as well as the establishment of unified command in the field.‡ When he came into office as Prime Minister he put these proposals into the forefront of his programme.

---

* *The World Crisis*, 1916–18, chapter x, p. 257.
† *Diplomacy by Conference* by Sir Maurice Hankey. Published in *The Round Table*, March 1922. *The War Memoirs* of David Lloyd George.
‡ *Memoirs* of David Lloyd George, vol. IV, p. 2386.

His first attempt to establish unified command early in 1917 by putting Sir Douglas Haig under the command of General Nivelle was a failure. Haig and Robertson detested the arrangement, and Nivelle and his Staff lacked the tact to overcome their objections.* Moreover, Nivelle's plan for an attack on the Chemin des Dames was allowed to leak out and resulted in a failure that had a disastrous effect on the morale of the French Army. General Sarrail's unified command of the allied armies in the Balkans also produced a lot of friction.

Mr Lloyd George, however, never relinquished the idea. In November 1917 he took advantage of the Italian collapse at Caporetto to rush down to Rapallo with M. Painlevé to meet the Italian Prime Minister and to 'put over' the plan of a Supreme War Council, which held its first meeting before the Conference adjourned. I acted as Secretary at this meeting—and of the whole Conference.

The Supreme War Council was immediately established at the Hotel Trianon, Versailles, with inter-allied permanent military representatives and a full staff for planning, and a permanent inter-allied secretariat, the British section of which was attached to the War Cabinet Office. I attended all the sessions of the Council as a Secretary.

The Supreme War Council, like all new institutions, had its teething troubles. But it became the focus of a vast inter-allied organisation, which included the Permanent Military Representatives, an allied Naval Council, the allied Maritime Transport Council, a Blockade Council, a Tank Committee and a network of inter-allied committees that had been built up gradually during the war to cover the whole field of inter-allied shipping, munitions, supply and war transport. It also eased the way for the unified command under Marshal Foch. The decisive step in this matter was actually taken by Lord Milner (who shared Mr Lloyd George's views on the subject) at a Conference at Doullens, held on 26th March 1918, under the shadow

* Brigadier-General Sir E. L. Spears, *Prelude to Victory*, chapter x.

of the German break-through east of Amiens. The system was amplified a little later at Conferences at Beauvais and Abbeville.

The best tribute to the success of these developments is that within almost exactly a year of the establishment of the Supreme War Council the last of the armistice conventions had been signed.

EARL LLOYD GEORGE

The gradual development of Government Control in the Great War 1914–18 by a system of trial and error has now been traced in three great spheres—the United Kingdom, the Empire and the Alliance. We owed much to Mr Asquith's solid spade-work, but in each sphere the system reached its maximum efficiency under the initiative of one man—David Lloyd George. I would ask my readers to think for a moment of what the nation owes to his leadership.

Around the bare bones of the story which I have merely sketched I would ask them to try and conjure up something of the greatness of the man: his burning patriotism; his courage and tenacity; his personal magnetism and the ascendancy that it gave him in Cabinet and Parliament alike; his unfailing resource; and, above all, his habit of snatching success out of adversity.

Thus, in the hour of our desperate need for war material in 1915, taking his political life in his hands, he founds the Ministry of Munitions. To the shattering German submarine campaign in 1917 he finds an antidote in the convoy system. Amid the chaos of Cabinet crisis in December 1916 he creates the War Cabinet system, which has ever since remained the central feature of Government Control in peace and war. By calling the Dominions and India to our counsels he paves the way for Empire and Commonwealth developments that have staggered the world. He seizes on the Italian disaster at Caporetto as the occasion to secure acceptance of the Supreme War Council, which prepares the way for the unified command within six months and victory within a year. And in the next chapter it will be seen that his reforms, so strenuously resisted and so hardly won, have been accepted during the present war as a matter of course and have become the foundation stones of our system to-day.

He is undoubtedly the founder of our modern system of Government Control in War, and for my part, as a witness and official recorder of these events, I wish to place on record my conviction that the man who won the war was David Lloyd George.

CHAPTER IV

BETWEEN THE WARS

IN the first two chapters the evolution of the Government Control in War has been traced from the establishment of the Committee of Imperial Defence at the beginning of the present century to the War Cabinet, Imperial War Cabinet and Supreme War Council of the last two years of the Great War of 1914–18.

Without claiming that perfection had been reached, it is justifiable to state that a satisfactory system had been evolved which was superior to that of our enemies or of any other nation in the previous history of war.

That system survives to this day in its main features, but during the interval between the two wars it was continually developed. Every year some embellishment was added, with the result that we were able to start the present war with a system, well tried in the last major war, but brought up to date and sufficiently flexible to be readily adapted to the ever-changing circumstances with which we were to be confronted.

ADMINISTRATIVE PREPARATION*

In 1916 Mr Asquith, and later Mr Lloyd George, had authorised an instruction to all Government Departments and organisations engaged in the war effort to record their experiences for use after the war in the compilation of a new War Book. Consequently there was plenty of material to work on.

In November 1919 the Committee of Imperial Defence was re-established. Two of the worst pre-war weaknesses, namely the absence of measures for dealing with man-power and supply, were met by the establishment of Committees known as the Man-Power Committee and the Principal Supply Officers' Committee to make all possible preparations on these important sub-

* The author's lecture at London University, March 1927. White Paper Statements on Defence, 1935–39, and Parliamentary Debates.

jects. Within the restrictions of a Pacifist policy both did invaluable work in preparing the man-power and supply arrangements for which the Ministry of Labour and National Service and the Ministry of Supply respectively became responsible before the outbreak of war in September 1939.

Most of the mushroom Government Departments that had sprung up during the war were abolished soon after its close, and were absorbed into parent Departments, which became responsible for preparation for war in these matters, forming nuclei for their expansion into new Government Departments in the event of war. In addition, the Committee of Imperial Defence set up a special Sub-Committee for each group of subjects, and permanent technical sections were attached to some Sub-Committees to work out various problems of detail.

The whole of these arrangements were supervised, as before 1914, by the Co-ordination Committee, which reported annually to the Committee of Imperial Defence on the state of this vast work of administrative preparation for war, as well as on the new War Book, which was kept continuously up to date as before 1914. By 1939 the arrangements were as good as, and in some respects an improvement on, those of 1914, within the limits of our policy.

ANCILLARIES TO AIR WARFARE

The development of air warfare had, of course, thrown up a number of new problems for settlement.

The planning for anti-aircraft defences was co-ordinated by the Home Defence Committee, and the Observer Corps was brought into existence. Later, their work was supplemented by a Committee of distinguished scientists to study the scientific aspects of the problem.* Among other things radiolocation, in which Sir Robert Watson-Watt played so important a part, was brought to light. It was a most opportune discovery and it was sufficiently developed by the outbreak of war to give us, among other things,

---

* Parliamentary Debates. Commons. 27th February 1935.

an effective warning system, and was of the greatest assistance in the Battle of Britain. Since then radiolocation has been developed to an extent that was only dimly discerned at the outset, and part of this development has been made public.

The Reports of the scientists were dealt with by a larger Sub-Committee of the Committee of Imperial Defence under the Minister for Co-ordination of Defence, which was responsible to the Committee of Imperial Defence for concerting the steps to be taken for putting the proposals into operation.[*]

Air-raid precautions were tackled as early as 1925 by a special Sub-Committee. The outline of the plan was completed in the 'twenties. A special Department was set up under the Home Office in April 1935,[†] and the innumerable details were worked up systematically to the complete scheme of Civil Defence that came into operation on the outbreak of war under Sir John Anderson, who had now become Home Secretary and Minister of Home Security.

The main difficulty in all this work was that, owing to our disarmament policy, and its reactions on financial policy, funds were not available to put the plans into operation. Paper plans are, of course, indispensable and invaluable, but there comes a time when they lack reality unless they can be put into operation even on a modest scale—a point that will be mentioned later. A beginning was made in 1935, but in many important matters very little progress was realised before 1936 or 1937, for the reason that our armaments industry had languished for lack of orders and large extensions were required.[‡] Nevertheless, there is no question that in 1939 the administrative preparations were as complete as they could be, *within the limits of our policy and the finances made available.*

We must now turn to developments in the organisation for policy and planning.

[*] Parliamentary Debates. Commons. 19th March and 6th June 1935.
[†] *Ibid.* 16th April 1935.
[‡] Statement relating to Defence, 3rd March 1936. (Cmd. 5107.)

POLICY AND PLANNING

Before the Great War 1914–18, planning at the political level, as we saw in the second chapter, was undertaken by a series of Ministerial Committees, often presided over by the Prime Minister himself, and including a few Ministers, the Service Chiefs of Staff and other experts, reporting to the Committee of Imperial Defence on such subjects as Invasion and Home Defence, the Continental problem, the defence of India, Egypt, etc. The accepted policy had then formed the basis of plans and preparations worked out in detail by the General Staffs of the Admiralty and War Office, Government Departments and Sub-Committees of the Committee of Imperial Defence.

THE AIR MINISTRY AND R.A.F.

During the war of 1914–18 a third Defence Department and a third Service had come into existence—the Air Ministry and the Royal Air Force. That involved great complications at first. The new Ministry and the new Air Force were very progressive. Like a Missionary Church they had to fight their way to equality of status against the prejudices of the older Services, and they pitched their claims very high. For example, they claimed that air forces should replace capital ships. The older Services reacted strongly against these claims and—especially the Navy—wanted to bring the organisation more into line with that of foreign nations, which for the most part had not adopted the system of a third Service. *

But the R.A.F. would have none of that. They attached decisive importance from the first to long-range strategical bombing, such as we have seen in the present war, and, in their view, the whole of the air services must be concentrated in one Service because the air was one. It was, they claimed, uneconomical to delegate parts of air warfare to other Departments and Services. If the

* Report of the Sub-Committee on National and Imperial Defence. (Cmd. 2029, 1924).

Royal Air Force was to be used at maximum efficiency, the Air Ministry must be free to allot its resources according to the needs of a war at all stages. Perhaps the Air Force claimed too much and was a trifle futurist (not a bad fault!), and perhaps the older Services offered too little. Only in July 1937 was it decided to transfer the administrative control of the Fleet Air Arm to the Admiralty.*

At any rate, in 1922 the situation was most embarrassing to the Committee of Imperial Defence, who, in many matters of policy and strategy, were constantly confronted with advice based on widely differing theories. It was necessary to find means to bring them into focus.

THE CHIEFS OF STAFF COMMITTEE

In 1923 the organisation of Imperial Defence was reviewed by a Sub-Committee of the Committee of Imperial Defence under Lord Salisbury.† Their most important recommendation was for the development of the Chiefs of Staff Committee, which Mr Lloyd George had established on a temporary footing during the Chanak crisis of 1922. The Salisbury Committee's Report consolidated the Committee and vastly increased its authority and status, which was laid down in the following key passage of the Report:

> In addition to the functions of the Chiefs of Staff as advisers on questions of sea, land or air policy respectively, to their own Board or Council, each of the three Chiefs of Staff will have an individual and collective responsibility for advising on defence policy as a whole, the three constituting, as it were, a Super-Chief of a War Staff in Commission. In carrying out this function they will meet together for the discussion of questions which affect their joint responsibilities.‡

The phrase 'a Super-Chief of a War Staff in Commission' was criticised at the time, but there was nothing new in the conception. The Board of Admiralty and the Army Council had

---

* Statement Relating to Defence Expenditure, 1938. (Cmd. 5682, para. 25.)
† Cmd. 2029, 1924.   ‡ *Ibid.*

long since put into commission the functions of the Lord High Admiral and the Commander-in-Chief of the Army respectively, and the Air Ministry had been organised from the first on lines corresponding to the Army Council. The Chiefs of Staff Committee merely extended the same principle into the sphere of inter-Services co-operation.

The Chairman of the Committee of Imperial Defence was to be *ex-officio* Chairman of the Chiefs of Staff Committee. The Salisbury Committee also recommended that the Prime Minister, who as President of the Committee of Imperial Defence had nearly always presided, should have a colleague as Deputy to assist him in the direction of the Committee of Imperial Defence, especially in what was termed the 'wider initiative', and to act as Chairman in his absence. Sometimes Prime Ministers appointed a Deputy; sometimes they preferred to take charge themselves, but on the establishment in 1936 of a Minister for Co-ordination of Defence he became *ex-officio* Deputy Chairman of both the Committee of Imperial Defence and the Chiefs of Staff Committee,* the Prime Minister remaining as Chairman. In practice it was found better to leave the Chiefs of Staff to work out by themselves their problems, which were mainly planning and operational, except when the Chairman, Deputy Chairman, or the Chiefs of Staff themselves thought otherwise—a system which has worked well in peace and war.

It is difficult to over-rate the great advance made by the establishment of the Chiefs of Staff Committee. Before long the succession of great sailors, soldiers and airmen who occupied the highest posts in the three Services had established a tradition of team-work, which has been particularly marked during the present war. They undertook the supervision and initiative in all planning, under the direction of the Committee of Imperial Defence, with its strong representation of Ministers. To assist them the already existing Home Defence Committee and Overseas Defence Committee, with their rather limited terms of

* Statement Relating to Defence, 3rd March 1936, para. 47. (Cmd. 5107.)

reference, were supplemented by a Joint Planning Committee (in 1927) and later a Joint Intelligence Committee, the latter presided over by a senior official of the Foreign Office, so that their plans could be worked out in detail in the light of all the information available to the Government. The Joint Planning Committee, consisting of the Directors of Plans of the three Service Departments, was supplemented by three officers, one from each Service, working under the Committee's direction on collective plans.*

For years before the war, therefore, the Chiefs of Staff were responsible for planning, with a standing inter-Services organisation to work out details, and under the immediate direction in matters of policy of a small Committee of Ministers and the general direction of the Committee of Imperial Defence.

That organisation was capable of conversion at a moment's notice into a system for Government Control by a War Cabinet advised by the Chiefs of Staff Committee, with its own inter-Services Planning and Intelligence organisations.

Besides dealing with planning and current questions, the Chiefs of Staff were responsible for a comprehensive annual review of our military situation as a whole in the light of the international situation as viewed by the Foreign Office.† That was a most important provision, for it ensured that the Cabinet, the Committee of Imperial Defence and the Foreign Office were kept apprised of our defensive situation.

THE SECRETARIAT

As Secretary of the Committee of Imperial Defence, I became the first Secretary of the Chiefs of Staff Committee with my Senior Assistant Secretary as Deputy. By that time I was also Secretary to the Cabinet and Clerk of the Privy Council and my services were often requisitioned as Secretary-General of

---

* Announcement by Prime Minister in Parliament, 27th February 1936.
† Parliamentary Debates. Commons. 22nd May 1935, vol. xxxii, col. 362.

International Conferences both at home and abroad, and of the Imperial Conferences held between the wars. But the Committee of Imperial Defence was my old love and always had first place in my thoughts, and my wider contacts gave me a very intimate knowledge of domestic and Empire and world developments bearing on the problem of Imperial Defence. I had the assistance of a succession of most able men, including at various times General Ismay, my successor as Secretary of the Committee of Imperial Defence, now Deputy Secretary of the War Cabinet and a member of the Chiefs of Staff Committee; Admiral Sir Henry Moore, afterwards Commander-in-Chief of the Home Fleet; General Sir Henry Pownall, until recently Chief of the General Staff to Lord Louis Mountbatten in South-East Asia; General Sir G. N. Macready, and Sir John Hodsoll, who has done so much for Civil Defence, and many others.

The Secretariat was still 'the corner-stone of the whole edifice', but the Chiefs of Staff Committee had become the power plant. The two were complementary.

On my retirement in 1938 a reorganisation took place. The Secretary of the Cabinet became the head of the Offices of the Cabinet and Committee of Imperial Defence with two deputies, styled respectively 'Clerk of the Privy Council and Deputy Secretary of the Cabinet' and 'Secretary of the Committee of Imperial Defence', but the tradition of team-work and close co-operation has been, and I believe always will be, maintained. The division of duties was a wise decision. In the threatening international situation the work of co-ordination of defence had widened out, and it would have been very difficult for a newcomer to control in detail the whole organisation, which had, so to speak, grown up with me.

THE IMPERIAL DEFENCE COLLEGE

One development that deserves special mention is the Imperial Defence College. Each Fighting Service, of course, had its own Staff College, but until after the foundation of the Chiefs of Staff Committee there was no educational establishment for the study of total war, the combined operations of the three Services and the problems of Higher Control.

The Imperial Defence College was founded in 1927 to fill this gap and Admiral Sir Herbert Richmond, now Master of Downing, was the first Commandant, working under the guidance of the Chiefs of Staff Committee. I wonder whether the Master of Downing realises how well he built!

The officers taking this post-graduate course were on average of the rank of Captain in the Navy, Colonel in the Army, and Group-Captain in the Royal Air Force. But a few Civil Servants also took part each year. Officers and occasionally Civil Servants were also sent to the course by the Dominions, India and the Colonies. The list includes some well-known figures of the present war, such as Admirals Sir Andrew Cunningham, Harwood, Moore, Power and Daniel; Generals the late Sir John Dill, Alan Brooke, Auchinleck, Paget, Ronald Adam, Pownall and Macready, and the Canadian Generals McNaughton and Crerar; Air Marshals Portal, Tedder, Evill, Park, the late Sir Trafford Leigh-Mallory, and Sir Frederick Shedden, the distinguished Secretary of the Australian Defence Department. The Imperial Defence College was a veritable nursery for leaders and their Chiefs of Staff, but we could have made use of many more graduates and it is to be hoped that after the war it will be reopened on a larger scale.

OBSERVATIONS

A question which obtrudes itself once more is why, with a system of planning for war that possessed so many merits, we were in 1939 once more caught by a great war in some respects even weaker, comparatively, than in 1914? That brings us to those issues of national policy which, as I have already hinted, dominated the whole situation and hampered us at every turn, and which are reserved for the last chapter. For the moment it is sufficient to record that both we and all the peace-loving nations were caught up by war with armaments totally insufficient both in numbers and efficiency to withstand the enemy. That brings us to the present war.

CHAPTER V

THE PRESENT WAR

IT is premature to judge the Government Control as a whole in the present war. Much is still obscure. We are too close to events for a proper perspective and the wars are not over. The ultimate results have been admirable, but slower in coming than in the last war. This is due mainly to the failure, just mentioned, of all the allied nations and all the peace-loving countries to provide adequate armaments, and perhaps in some degree also to the fallibility of human judgment, against which no system can provide. There is little doubt that, as in the last war, shipping losses have proved our greatest handicap, and in spite of the recent recovery, tonnage is still difficult, though not calamitous.

But it is not desired to overstress that aspect. 'He who has made no mistakes in war', said Turenne, 'has made little war.' In the complicated business of allotting our total resources, especially before they are fully developed, between many claimants, combined with all the imponderabilia of war, it is easy to make mistakes, especially in balancing and synchronising naval, military and air programmes that have to be laid down years before their completion. If against our setbacks we put our long series of successes in all theatres by sea, land and air, the balance is heavily in favour of the excellence of our system.

GOVERNMENT CONTROL AT HOME

On the outbreak of war, in accordance with arrangements planned long beforehand, the Committee of Imperial Defence was suspended and a War Cabinet was established to which the Chiefs of Staff became responsible. The newcomers were Mr Churchill and myself.

The new War Cabinet, inheriting from the Committee of Imperial Defence of 1904, was based on Mr Lloyd George's system, brought up to date, as already explained, by the establishment of the Chiefs of Staff Committee and the Joint Planning and Joint Intelligence organisations behind it; with machinery for man-power and supply which, though far from perfect, was an improvement on the last war; and with very complete arrangements for the transition of the whole machinery of Government from a state of peace to a state of war, which worked without a hitch. The Cabinet and Committee of Imperial Defence Secretariat were merged into a single War Cabinet Secretariat.

The members of the new War Cabinet had, for the most part, been associated in the planning arrangements and could be under no illusions as to the limitations of the Allies.

Owing to our own weakness and that of the French, especially in the air, there was nothing we could do to save Poland, whose fate could only depend on the ultimate outcome of the war and our ability to bring about the eventual defeat of Germany. Victory requires the concentration of decisive force at the decisive point and at the decisive moment. The Allies did not dispose of decisive force, the decisive point was out of reach, and the decisive moment had not come—and, as most of us foresaw—could not come for years. The enemy, owing to greater readiness, had the initiative and in the early months we had to concentrate all our efforts on building up our strength to meet the situation when the curtain fell on the Polish tragedy. When the clash came, we still lacked the power to save Norway, Denmark, Holland, Belgium or even France, though we took grave risks to support her with all the strength we could spare and more. But between the beginning of rearmament in 1935 and the collapse of France in 1940 we just succeeded in accumulating sufficient force to avert our own collapse, thanks largely to the imperishable gallantry of the Royal Air Force in the Battle of Britain. That was part of Mr Chamberlain's much under-rated contribution.

After the failure to save Norway the Government changed; Italy had come into the war; and we were threatened in the Mediterranean, Egypt and the Suez Canal, the jugular vein of the British Empire. The War Cabinet was reconstituted on a party basis and included several members without knowledge of our preparations for war and without experience of its conduct. In those circumstances, while the ultimate responsibility for the conduct of the war rested with the War Cabinet, with the Chiefs of Staff as their professional advisers, the Prime Minister assumed the additional title of Minister of Defence, and superintended on behalf of the War Cabinet the work of the Chiefs of Staff Committee, that is to say, control of Planning and Operations (as distinct from higher war policy and strategy), assisted by a Defence Committee over which he himself presided and which includes the Deputy Prime Minister (Mr Attlee), Foreign Secretary, Minister of Production, the three Service Ministers, the Chiefs of Staff and the Chief of Combined Operations. *

The powers of the Prime Minister as Minister of Defence are not laid down in any statute or other legal instrument, but are virtually inherent in the office in time of war, though the manner in which those powers are exercised varies with the individual and the circumstances. In 1940, when we were threatened with invasion, those circumstances were very grave. Mr Churchill has described the system as follows:

While, as I have said, I take constitutional responsibility for everything that is done or not done, and am quite ready to take the blame myself when things go wrong...I do not, of course, conduct this war from day to day myself; it is conducted from day to day, and in its future outlook, by the Chiefs of Staff Committee, namely, the First Sea Lord, the Chief of the Imperial General Staff, and the Chief of the Air Staff. These officers sit together every day, and often twice a day. They give executive directions and orders to the Commanders-in-Chief in the various theatres.

* The Organisation for Joint Planning. (Cmd. 6351, 1942.)

They advise me, they advise the Defence Committee and the War Cabinet on large questions of war strategy and war policy.*

Mr Churchill mentioned also that in 1941, out of 462 meetings of the Chiefs of Staff Committee, he only presided at 44 himself. In a later statement on 2nd July 1942, generally confirming the earlier statement, he added that he himself worked under the supervision of the War Cabinet to whom all important matters were referred and whom he had to carry with him in all major decisions.†

As to relations with Commanders-in-Chief, he said (2nd July) that the policy was 'not to worry them but to leave them alone to do their job', subject to occasional 'messages of encouragement and sometimes a query or a suggestion, but it is absolutely impossible to fight battles from Westminster or Whitehall. The less one interferes the better....'‡

It will be noticed that those statements correspond exactly to the basic principles suggested in earlier chapters, though the methods differ in some respects from those of the last war, and the application of the principles is liable to differ according to the temperament of the individual.

Mr Churchill brought to the task an experience greater than any of his predecessors as a combatant, a war correspondent, a historian of mediaeval and modern war, as First Lord of the Admiralty in both the Great Wars, as a Minister of Munitions, a Secretary of State for War and Air, a member of the War Council and Dardanelles Committee in the last war and of the War Cabinet at the outset of the present war.

Machiavelli declared that 'A Prince ought to have no other aim or thought, nor select anything else for his study, than war and its rules and discipline'. Mr Churchill, however, brought much more than that to his task—unsurpassed political and Parliamentary experience, superb gifts of oratory and popular leadership, as well as long views, great resolution, a vast capacity for

* Parliamentary Debates. Commons. 24th February 1942.
† *Ibid.*   ‡ *Ibid.*

work, and above all, immense physical and moral courage. The memory of his leadership will live for ever.

To realise the difficulties, try to picture a few of the problems of the Supreme Command during the present war. Think, for example, what forethought was required, when the Mediterranean was closed to our shipping, to plan and prepare for an operation in North Africa which could not begin until six months later or more, as both troops and stores had to be carried round Africa by ships in convoy subjected to U-boat attack all the way. Consider the advance arrangements for the enlargement of existing ports in Egypt and other parts of the Middle East, the provision of new ones, and of labour and rail and road communications to serve them, of aerodromes with fuel, workshops and all the other accessories, as well as anti-aircraft artillery, searchlights, balloons and so forth. Picture the problem of weighing the risks in allocating in early days our exiguous naval, military and air resources between home defence, including anti-aircraft defence, anti-U-boat warfare, Russia, North Africa and the Mediterranean, the Middle East (at one time gravely threatened) and the Far East. Coming to later days, try to imagine the planning and preparation for the culminating triumph of 'D' Day. Add the exasperating but often unavoidable delays in the output of war material or shipping transport, or some vital necessity like landing craft, or some heartbreaking loss at sea or failure on the field of battle. Do not overlook the provision of food for our own population, raw materials for our war industries; economic pressure on the enemy; negotiations with neutrals; the building-up over years of the partisan and underground warfare, which has proved so valuable in the later stages.

Add to all that the need for concerting everything with the Dominions, India—to say nothing of the Colonies—and especially our major Allies, from whom we were separated by vast distances, and you will get some faint conception of the problems and anxieties that beset the military side of our Government Control at all stages of the war. I think you will agree that the machine has stood up to it astonishingly well. In essence, it remained an adaptation of the Lloyd George model with the addition of the Chiefs of Staff Committee and its planning organisation as designed between the wars, and at a higher level the Defence Committee and War Cabinet, the whole being under the control of the Prime Minister.

Of course, there have been embellishments and adjustments, modifications and a huge expansion to meet the world-wide spread of the war: for instance, the establishment by Mr Chamberlain of the Committee of Vice-Chiefs of Staff to take some of the weight off the Chiefs of Staff, and the strengthening and expansion of the Planning and Intelligence organisations. All this has produced a Chiefs of Staff organisation to-day which is the best example the world has ever known of a great Joint General Staff to cover and combine all aspects of inter-Service operations.

ADMINISTRATIVE CONTROL

The Prime Minister's preoccupation in the military side of the war, especially when his long, exhausting but necessary and courageous absences abroad on inter-allied affairs are taken into account, renders it physically impossible for him, in spite of his exceptional powers of work, to give as much attention as did Mr Lloyd George to the many important administrative matters remaining for the War Cabinet.

Moreover, the structure of the War Cabinet itself appears from outside to be less adapted for relieving the burden of work by the method of delegation adopted by Mr Lloyd George, since there are no War Cabinet Ministers comparable with Lord Curzon, Lord Milner or General Smuts without heavy departmental and/or Parliamentary duties to deal with the many interdepartmental questions that must arise. Resort, however, can always be made to the peace-time expedient of delegation to Cabinet Committees, some of which are standing bodies and others appointed *ad hoc.*

Personally I think that on the administrative side the more flexible system adopted in the last war, which was described in Chapter II, is preferable. It is very important that those members of the War Cabinet on whom rests the main responsibility for administrative decisions bearing on the war effort should be in very close touch with the military side, in order that they may be in a position to take long views in meeting the coming needs of the Fighting Services. For example, in a total war such as the present one, it is obvious that the plans for handling the requirements of the civilian populations in liberated or occupied territories require to be dovetailed very carefully, particularly in matters of supplies, shipping and land transport, into those of the military authorities, since the contentment and, if possible, active co-operation of those peoples may be of the utmost importance to the war effort. Here civilian members of the War Cabinet can make a real contribution if they are sufficiently informed. Maybe they are.

However this may be, the system as a whole—military and civilian—has produced such remarkable results that we ought not to be too critical.

THE EMPIRE AND COMMONWEALTH*

Between the wars Empire co-operation in Defence was provided by four methods:

(i) The periodical meetings of the Imperial Conference, at which the subject of Imperial Defence was invariably discussed in all its aspects. At the Conference of 1923, for example, principles of co-operation on questions of common defence were drawn up, which were reaffirmed and extended at the Conference of 1926.

(ii) The co-operation of the Dominions, each in its own way, in the work of the Committee of Imperial Defence and its numerous Sub-Committees. Some Dominions regularly exer-

* 'The War Effort of the Dominions.' *The Nineteenth Century and After* (July 1943), Lord Hankey.

cised their right of representation at the Committee by their High Commissioners.*

(iii) The appointment of liaison officers to the General Staffs of the three Services in London, interchanges of Staff Officers, attendance of Dominions officers at the Imperial Defence College and the Service Staff Colleges, etc.

(iv) The communication of a stream of documents giving the Dominions full knowledge of what we were doing and enabling them to make arrangements appropriate to their own circumstances.

When, at the outset of the present war, Canada, Australia, New Zealand and South Africa decided to participate with the United Kingdom in the fight for freedom, their Prime Ministers were too busy for a long time with their respective war efforts to attend an Imperial Conference. This did not really matter, as discussions at Imperial Conferences had been so thorough, the exchange of views and information had become so regular, and the system of inter-communication at all levels, both on policy and detail, was so complete that few major difficulties arose. Moreover, since the autumn of 1939 there has been a long succession of visits by individual Prime Ministers and other Ministers, who usually attended meetings of the War Cabinet during their stay and kept their respective Governments well informed of the military and political situation and outlook. These visits were supplemented by the invaluable work of the High Commissioners who meet daily with the Secretary of State for Dominion Affairs, as well as of naval, military, air, scientific and other missions and liaison officers.

It was not until May 1944 that the Prime Ministers of the Dominions were all able to meet with Mr Churchill in London, and that was only for a short session as compared with the meetings of the Imperial War Cabinet in the last war.†

---

* Mr Bruce, who has done much for Empire co-operation, was a frequent attendant for many years before the war. He represents the Commonwealth of Australia at the War Cabinet.

† Since the Lees Knowles Lectures there have been further meetings in connection with the San Francisco Conference (April, 1945).

Nevertheless, for the reasons given above, this co-ordination of the Empire's war effort, if less spectacular, has not been less effective than in the last war.

What could be more impressive for example than the manner in which the Dominions combined with us in naval operations the world over, in the Battle of Britain, in the Battle of the Atlantic, in North Africa, and in the Invasion of Europe? We can never over-rate that assistance. We can never forget, in particular, how Australia and New Zealand came to our aid at a time when they themselves had hanging over them the dire threat of Japanese aggression, and we have promised to repay it in the coming onslaught in the Pacific.

INTER-ALLIED CO-OPERATION

At the outset of the war a Supreme War Council was established between the British and French Governments. Air communications enabled frequent meetings to take place without difficulty between the Prime Ministers and other representatives of the two Governments, accompanied by their respective Chiefs of Staff and other experts, as well as between the experts themselves. In these circumstances no organisation comparable to the Versailles arrangements of 1917 was found necessary. In the field of supply and transport, however, a very complete system was devised before the war and came into full existence on its outbreak.

After the collapse of France and the intervention of Russia and the United States the situation was much more difficult owing to the vast distances involved.

Once more the development of air communications provided the solution, and effective combined control at the highest level was established between the Western Allies by the numerous meetings between President Roosevelt, Mr Churchill and Marshal Stalin, sometimes two at a time and occasionally three at a time, as at Teheran and the recent Crimea Conference. Once also, Generalissimo Chiang-Kai-Shek came into conference with the Western Allies at Cairo.

In addition a permanent Combined Staff, with a planning organisation and secretariat attached, was set up long ago in Washington, which works very much on the lines of our own Chiefs of Staff organisation, and has been astonishingly successful in concerting planning arrangements. It is from Washington, of course, that the brilliant and successful operations of the Pacific War are mainly directed, and it is obvious that, except in South-East Asia, the South-West Pacific and Australasia, the main initiative must rest with our American Allies. Russia, it is understood, has not been represented on the Combined Staff at Washington, but at the Crimea Conference arrangements were made for military co-operation between the Powers concerned in the last stages of the invasion of Germany.

Besides this, elaborate arrangements of a most complete character have grown up between all the Allies on questions of supply, transport, etc., which it would be impossible to describe within the limits of these chapters.

Finance has been provided, of course, by the Lend-Lease system, which has enabled us to avoid the terrible financial embarrassments of the last war.

POLITICAL CONTROL

On the political side of Allied control the outstanding feature is that the three Principal Powers have succeeded in holding together; there has been criticism on some issues—Poland, for example—but current political controversy is beyond our subject.

Perhaps the right solution has been found in the strengthening of the existing machinery by more frequent meetings of Foreign Ministers as arranged at the Crimea Conference—a system that I favoured in the last war.

OBSERVATIONS

The story of Government Control in the present war has now been brought up to date (March 1945). Taking it as a whole; allowing for the world-wide scale of the war, the paucity of our original preparations, the vast size of the forces in the three elements of sea, land and air, the novel problems that had to be solved, the rapid march of science and some mistakes, we cannot, I think, reach any conclusion other than it is a very good story, reflecting the greatest credit on all concerned. The main point is that we are winning the war! But it is not yet over, especially in the Pacific, where we have a long way to go. So we must keep up the pressure.

CHAPTER VI

SOME CRITICISMS EXAMINED

THE matters which it was possible to include within the time limits of the Lees Knowles Lectures have now been covered, but it may be useful to comment on some of the criticisms that have been made against the system described above and to add a few observations of a general nature.

THE 'PERNICIOUS COMMITTEE SYSTEM'

There are some who hold that our system of preparation for and control of war is radically unsound. It is sometimes roundly condemned as a pernicious means of avoiding or delaying decisions and shifting responsibility. The supposed revival after the last war of the Committee system has been contrasted adversely with the vigorous conduct of the last war by the small War Cabinet under Mr Lloyd George.

In this respect, however, the critics are misinformed. The War Cabinet, which was, of course, itself a Committee, inherited and greatly extended the Committee system of its predecessors, and by the end of the war the number must have been between 150 and 200. For example, there were no less than 45 inter-allied Committees focusing ultimately into the Supreme War Council. After the re-establishment of the Committee of Imperial Defence the number was much reduced. No figures have been published of the number of Committees to-day, but it would be a fair guess that they are not less than in the last war. The systems in war and peace are virtually the same, except that in war the *tempo* is increased.

The fact is that there is in the last resort no alternative to Committees for the prompt despatch of business where the action of a number of different executive authorities has to be combined. Somehow or other the representatives of those who have to take action have to be got together round a table, conflicting difficulties have to be adjusted, and action concerted in an ordered sequence. The easiest way of doing this is to bring the parties together into a Committee.

Take, for example, a simple illustration—the despatch of supplies to a great ally, of which we have had much experience in the last and in the present war.

First the requirement has to be ascertained from the ally over a range of perhaps hundreds of items. Resources are not unlimited and the demands of other users—our own Navy, Army and Air Force, the civilian population, the Dominions, India and the Colonies and other allies—have to be ascertained and put into an order of priority. The stocks available, the present and future capacity of output, and the possibilities of expansion have then to be ascertained from the supply departments concerned, who themselves have to weigh up such matters as manufacturing capacity, machine tools, raw materials and labour (which brings in another Department, the Ministry of Labour). On these data a programme can be laid out. Next comes the transport of all this material by land and sea, and if shipping tonnage is tight, that may give the Ministry of Transport a difficult problem. The capacity of the ports of embarkation and of disembarkation, and of the railways serving them then comes into the picture. Often they require huge works to enable them to handle the programme. Then there come an Admiralty problem—the provision of escorts for the protection of the convoys—and a closely connected Air Force problem—the provision of air cover.

In order to ensure that all those processes are properly examined, mistakes avoided, and the whole embodied rapidly in a concerted programme designed to avoid all possible delay, it is absolutely necessary to get together the representatives of every section concerned, so that each of them understands the plan into which he has to fit and exactly the part he has to play, and the dates at which he must be ready to take action. And the programme must be watched from day to day to ensure that nothing gets behind-hand.

That means a Committee and perhaps Sub-Committees and

Conferences as well. It is sheer nonsense to say that this means delay and passing on responsibility. A good chairman, who must of course be well acquainted with the policy of the War Cabinet, will never tolerate that. He will watch the situation every day, ever on the look out for a hitch, finding a solution for every difficulty, never allowing matters to stand still. He must also have a first-rate and prompt secretariat to act as his executive.

That is how Mr Lloyd George and his colleagues worked in the last war and their successors in the present war. Even in cases where questions were delegated to one or more members of the War Cabinet they had to proceed by calling into Conference or Committee those responsible for action in order to concert their arrangements.

Of course, the meetings must be carefully prepared for, fully documented, and often preceded by personal consultations so that all may go rapidly and smoothly. The truth is that the Committee system is only pernicious when it is badly run.

The supposed superman, who thinks he knows everything, refuses to call into counsel those who know the details and issues slapdash orders without proper investigation, usually lands his country and himself in a dreadful mess. The result often is great confusion. The right hand of the Government does not know what the left hand is doing. Order, counter-order and disorder follow. That is where the Dictators have failed. No enemy operation has approached the perfection of far-sighted planning and execution achieved on 'D' Day. We owe that to the concerted action of the Heads of Governments at their periodical meetings in Committee, the Combined Staff, working in Committee in Washington, the War Cabinet system, and especially the Chiefs of Staff Committee in London. To these must be added the brilliant work of the Commanders-in-Chief of the British and American Navies, Armies and Air Forces under General Eisenhower, and, of course, the valour and efficiency of the Forces, which result in large degree from well-concerted training and rehearsal.

It would be a great mistake to make any fundamental alteration in a system that has served us so well, although, of course, changes in detail will probably be made as the result of war experience as they were after 1914–18.

A COMBINED GENERAL STAFF

The demand is sometimes made that we should substitute a Combined General Staff for our present system.

It is difficult to discover exactly what is intended by a Combined General Staff, or how it differs from our present system.

The principal functions of a General Staff are Planning, Operations, Intelligence and Training. In the case of a Combined General Staff, planning and operations obviously require Staff Officers with up-to-date knowledge of the sea, land and air aspects of their problems. They will only be up to date if they have had recent experience, as warfare moves very fast, and have kept in touch with all new and prospective developments. That is exactly what our present system provides for. In the Joint Planning and Operational Sections officers of various ranks work continuously together and even live together. Some have been, and it is hoped that all in future will be, trained together at the Imperial Defence College. But even to-day these teams of workers in continuous contact have acquired a unique knowledge of how to handle the joint problems of the three Services.

Of course, after joint planning is complete, there is an immense amount of preparation required by each Fighting Service, and each requires its own General Staff to work out details. It is essential therefore that the Joint Planners should have the closest contact with the General Staffs of the three Services, and for that reason even the officers who work permanently together in the Chiefs of Staff organisation usually have rooms or desks in the Admiralty, War Office or Air Ministry.

Wider contacts are provided by liaison officers with the Ministry of War Transport, the Ministry of Economic Warfare, the Political Warfare Executive, the Ministry of Home Security, and other Departments when necessary.

The Joint Intelligence organisation, which feeds the Joint Planning organisation, is run on somewhat similar lines, but is presided over by a senior Foreign Office official and includes a second representative of the Foreign Office and two representatives of the Ministry of Economic Warfare.

The whole organisation, of course, works under the direction of the Chiefs of Staff, who are themselves guided in matters of policy by the Defence Committee and the War Cabinet, with the Prime Minister in the conning tower.

The highly experienced War Cabinet Secretariat provides a connecting link for the whole organisation, civil and military, and is an indispensable factor in co-ordination.

That is at any rate a reasonable conception of a Combined or Joint General Staff, and it has proved its worth. As described in earlier chapters, it can be rapidly changed from a war system into a peace system, and *vice versa* from a peace system to serve the needs of war. In a phrase, the reply to the critics on this point is that we already possess a Combined Staff.

THE HUMAN FACTOR

In the last resort efficiency always depends on the human factor, on comradeship, easy relations and team-work.

One valuable result of the system that has grown up in the last forty years is a gradual change in the relations between Ministers and public servants. When I joined the Naval Intelligence Department in 1901 there was a good story going about that, shortly after the first installation of the telephone in the Foreign Office, one of the higher officials was summoned to the new instrument to speak to the Secretary of State. Before doing so, however, he put on the ceremonial frock-coat which was *de rigueur* in an interview with the Minister! Whether the story was true or not, it illustrates the greater formality which used to prevail between Ministers and officials.

The increasing *tempo* of Government business, however, which has resulted from modern developments has brought about great changes in these relations.

Sir Victor Wellesley, late Deputy Under-Secretary of State for Foreign Affairs, has assembled some remarkable evidence on this subject in his recent book.* As late as 1893 the functions of the Foreign Office staff were purely clerical and confined almost entirely to matters of routine. Even the Permanent Under-Secretary had no higher duty than that of superintending the clerical work.

Sir Thomas Sanderson, as late as 1906, was criticised because he never offered an opinion on policy to the Secretary of State: my belief is that he would not have regarded it as his duty to do so. Up to 1906 the Foreign Office, meaning the permanent staff, had not the significance it then began to obtain.†

To illustrate the pressure on Ministers a remark is quoted by Sir Edward Grey that 'during his term of office he was so pressed that he could not remember having taken any step that was not of immediate urgency and for the solving of a problem directly in front of him'.‡

The inevitable result has been a much greater dependence of Ministers on officials. 'The staff of the Foreign Office then ceased to be purely clerical and executive and became largely advisory.'

As the volume and complexity of work increased and became more highly specialised, the drive which used to come exclusively from the top downwards, tended to come more and more from below upwards. Thus the initiation of high policy fell increasingly into the hands of the staff, often into those of very junior members, who had become experts on a particular subject.... That the Foreign Secretary must be briefed, and that this is the job of the permanent officials goes without saying....

---

* Sir Victor Wellesley, *Diplomacy in Fetters*, 1944, chapter xiv.
† Quoted by Sir Victor Wellesley from Sir John Tilley and Sir Stephen Gaselee, *The Foreign Office*.
‡ Hugh Wilson, *Education of the Diplomat*, chapter iv, p. 47.

The same thing was happening in other Government Depart-ments. I witnessed it myself inside the Admiralty between 1901 and 1906.

In that humanising process the Committee of Imperial Defence and its numerous Sub-Committees played a considerable part. Meeting together round a table week after week Ministers, Staff Officers and Civil Servants got to know one another, to respect one another and to like one another. Statesmen and fighting men learned a lot of each other's problems, which was very useful when war came upon us. '*Tout comprendre, c'est tout pardonner.*' Suspicion melted away and often enough friendship took its place. Not only between Ministers and other public servants, but also between Government Departments, the formal and some-times rather frigid relations gave way to personal contacts.

That is not the least of the advantages we owe to the present system. Undoubtedly it has strengthened discipline, loyalty and team-work.

CHAPTER VII

THE FUTURE

PRINCIPLES

THE subject of Government Control in War has now been explored through two major wars and their preparation. The governing principles may be summed up as follows:

(i) Control in war must remain in the hands of statesmen, working in the closest co-operation with the Service Chiefs.

(ii) The Prime Minister of the day is 'the keystone of the Cabinet arch', and he alone must be the head of the Government Control in time of war.

(iii) In the grand strategy of the war the views of the Service Chiefs must usually prevail, but even here the last word must rest with the statesmen, who are responsible for policy and for distributing the resources of the country in the manner best calculated to win the war.

(iv) Relations between statesmen and Commanders-in-Chief should be conducted on the principle that, having selected the best men available, they should be given a free hand and backed up to the hilt with a minimum of interference. That principle should rarely be departed from, but in the last resort statesmen are entitled and bound to step in, e.g. to preserve the staying power of the State or Alliance, or in the interests of some equally essential operation elsewhere, or in the event of a difference of opinion between the leaders of the different Services or different Allied Nations.

(v) Governments are entitled to ask their Commanders-in-Chief to consider alternative plans to their own, but should rarely ask them to carry out plans in which they do not believe.

(vi) In time of peace the Prime Minister, whether with or without the assistance of a Deputy, should always be responsible for and well acquainted with our preparations for war. Some of his colleagues should be associated with him in this.

It has been shown that the above principles were observed very closely in practice by Mr Asquith and Mr Lloyd George in the last war and by Mr Chamberlain and Mr Churchill in the present war, and that for 40 years our Prime Ministers, as Presidents of the Committee of Imperial Defence, have been responsible for preparations for war.

METHODS

Leaving fundamental principles and coming to methods of exercising Government Control, it has been suggested:

(*a*) That the least satisfactory system of Control in War was by a large Cabinet of peace-time dimensions, which has been discarded since December 1916.

(*b*) That Government Control by a War Council or War Committee subordinate to a Cabinet of peace-time dimensions, although much more satisfactory than the peace-time Cabinet alone, involved divided responsibility and was therefore dangerous.

(*c*) That the most successful form of Government Control in War has been by a small War Cabinet composed of a few Ministers of great experience, some of them, if possible, free from Ministerial or heavy Parliamentary duties, and able to give their whole time to the central problems of the war, and to lift some of the weight off the Prime Minister.

ADDITIONAL CONCLUSIONS

Experience suggests the following additional conclusions:

(1) That, as a matter of principle, over-riding the above if necessary, the Prime Minister, as head of the Government Control, must have the system and organisation that his methods and temperament and the circumstances of the times require. Machines are made for men and not men for machines.

(2) The system must be extremely flexible so as to be adaptable to different temperaments and circumstances.

One of the greatest merits of our present system is its flexibility, which is one of the main reasons of its success.

BACK TO THE COMMITTEE OF IMPERIAL DEFENCE

Coming to the future of Government Control in War the present system both in peace and war is based on perfectly sound principles and is sufficiently flexible for adjustment to any new conditions that may arise. Its working is well understood by all

Government Departments concerned in National Defence and by the Governments of the Dominions and India, and it has seen us successfully through one and nearly through the second of two of the greatest major wars in our history. Whatever else is done, therefore, the Committee of Imperial Defence, including, of course, the whole of the Chiefs of Staff organisation, must be adopted as the basis of our future arrangements.

That is to say, there should be a transition, whenever circumstances permit, from the War Cabinet back to the Committee of Imperial Defence, which should at once begin to build up our war arrangements for the future in concert with any long- or short-term mutual security arrangements into which we may enter. The system is so devised that the transition from a war footing to a peace footing should present no difficulties, although, owing to the upheaval of the present war, the process may have to be very gradual.

SCIENCE AND ENGINEERING

As compared with the pre-war system one most important new development will have to be a much greater use of science in all its branches, including engineering and other applied sciences.

A most important part of our central system must be a strong scientific and engineering section to watch all developments in physics, chemistry and explosives, civil, mechanical, electrical and chemical engineering, metallurgy, biology, nutrition, medicine, etc., from the point of view of their possible use by an enemy and ourselves; to plan the measures to be taken to neutralise new developments and to lay out research.

Very little is known to the public as yet of the decisive influence that modern scientific developments have had on our naval, military and air operations, much of which has still to be kept secret for security reasons. Some of the expected measures of frightfulness such as gas warfare were not resorted to—possibly because it was known that we had prepared against them before the war—but the famous Cambridge scientists would agree that the potentialities of modern science and the recent developments in many fields suggest the possibility that methods of warfare are more than ever liable to change in the post-war years. There may even be new developments before the end of the present war.

After the war, therefore, scientific work on defence should be brought to the centre and co-ordinated by a special organisation attached to the Committee of Imperial Defence. This might include a small directing Committee, perhaps on the lines of the existing Scientific and Engineering Advisory Committees, with a large panel of consultants, and a Secretariat composed of whole-time specialists: in short, a sub-organisation very similar to the organisation of the parent body of which it will form a most important part.

Each Government Department concerned in Imperial Defence will, of course, have its own Scientific Division as at present,* closely linked up to the central body.

A corollary to this is the organisation of scientists in advance for war emergency and the inclusion in our war arrangements of plans for expansion, and training of the huge numbers required.

UNPREPAREDNESS

There remains the question, which has been reserved to this final chapter, of how we are to ensure against a repetition of the dangers of entering the war with totally inadequate forces, which brought us near to disaster in 1914 and even nearer in 1940.

In entering on that thorny ground it must be emphasised that in both cases the risks we ran were due at least as much to the deficiencies of our Allies as of ourselves.

THE CAUSES

First we ought to seek the causes of our deficiencies. These are stated clearly and succinctly in the following extract from the first of the Annual Statements on Defence issued by the National

---

* Scientific Research and Development. (Cmd. 6514, 1944.)

Government in March 1935 (Cmd. 4827), to warn the nation of the coming dangers:

During the years that all parties in this country have been seeking to carry out the policy outlined above,* there has been a steady decline in the effective strength of our armaments by sea and land. In the air we virtually disarmed ourselves in 1919, and, subsequently, from time to time postponed attainment of the minimum air strength regarded as necessary to our security in the face of air developments on the Continent. It is not that British Governments have neglected to keep themselves informed of the position. Every year the state of our armaments has been anxiously considered, and if risks have been run they have been accepted deliberately in pursuit of the aim of permanent peace. Again and again, rather than run any risk of jeopardising some promising movement in this direction by increasing expenditure on armaments, Governments have postponed the adoption of measures that were required when considered from the point of view of national defence alone. In this way we have taken risks for peace, but, as intimated by the Secretary of State for Foreign Affairs in the debate on the Address on the 28th November, 1934 'disarming ourselves in advance, by ourselves, by way of an example—has not increased our negotiating power in the Disarmament discussions at Geneva.

'Parliament and people, however, have been warned again and again that serious deficiencies were accumulating in all the Defence Services, and that our desire to lead the world towards disarmament by our example of unilateral disarmament has not succeeded. We have not contributed thereby to general disarmament, and are approaching a point when we are not possessed of the necessary means of defending ourselves against an aggressor.'

That passage explains why we were again inadequately armed in 1939. It is the old, old story. It is admitted that successive Governments were aware of the dangers and it is made clear that this was passed on to Parliament and people, and that the risks were run deliberately in pursuit of the aim of permanent peace. The root cause then was the same as in 1914, as described in the first chapter, namely our traditional policy of peace, carried this time to the verge of risk and beyond. Not only were our forces

* A policy of peace and disarmament.

too small for safety, not only were they inadequately supplied, but the armaments industry, on which they depended, the nucleus on which the war supply arrangements had to be founded, had been gravely impaired by lack of orders from home and abroad in the decade after the war. Even the acceptance of orders from foreign countries was rigidly controlled. The result was that many skilled men disappeared and when rearmament began in 1935 we were frightfully handicapped. It is a curious commentary that during 1935 and 1936 a Royal Commission was investigating the prohibition of the private manufacture of arms, throwing an immense burden on those very Government Departments that required all their time and energy for rearmament.

All that reveals the truth that our unpreparedness in 1939 resulted from a failure not of our system of Imperial Defence but of the political working of our constitutional system of Government by Parliament and people.

SUGGESTIONS EXAMINED

Several proposals have been made for providing against this danger. One of the most interesting is Admiral of the Fleet Lord Chatfield's suggestion in the House of Lords on 28th March 1944,* for the creation of a National Defence Council to be presided over by the Prime Minister and including a strong nucleus of the Ministers concerned in Foreign Policy and Defence, as well as the Leaders of the Opposition Parties, with representatives of the Dominions if they should so desire, to concert a long-range programme and keep an eye on its development. Lord Chatfield supplemented his original proposals by some further suggestions made in the House of Lords on 7th March 1945.

While accepting the principle I would prefer the use of the Committee of Imperial Defence to a new and separate National Defence Council. Otherwise the Committee of Imperial Defence, with its powerful organisation and high prestige, would lose something of its status, and there is a danger of overlap

* Described more comprehensively in Lord Chatfield's pamphlet *Defence after the War* (Cassell).

between the two bodies. Precedents for the association of Opposition Leaders in the work of the Committee of Imperial Defence have been mentioned in these chapters, e.g. Lord Balfour's connection with the Invasion question before the war, and many other instances occurred between the wars. There is therefore no constitutional difficulty in carrying out Lord Chatfield's plan or the above variant thereof, provided the Opposition Leaders are willing to take part.

Those plans might in favourable circumstances go some way towards securing continuity of policy, unless and until defence— or foreign policy which is closely associated with defence— became a major party issue, and in that event it would fall into abeyance for a time, though not necessarily for ever.

There is substance, however, in Lord Chatfield's contention that the scale of our defences must not be tied too closely to foreign policy. Experience shows that Allies cannot always fulfil their commitments. They may have internal or external embarrassments that prevent them, such as Presidential or General Elections or Colonial wars. They may be completely unready or public opinion may be opposed to war. We are looking forward hopefully to international schemes, partially evolved at Dumbarton Oaks, to be completed at San Francisco, for keeping the peace, but the history of previous efforts, and especially the tragic failure of the League of Nations, enjoins caution. At any rate, while doing all we can to make the new system a success, it would be as well to keep our powder dry.

Apart from possible disagreement on foreign policy, however, there are other difficulties in carrying out Lord Chatfield's proposal. The cost of modern armaments is enormous, and every penny spent on armaments leaves a penny less for essential reconstruction, housing and other social reforms. Political leaders, it has been pointed out, would find it difficult to agree to very costly armament programmes if they found that they would postpone to the Greek Kalends reforms to which they were pledged at a General Election.

The antidote to that is Lord Chatfield's proposal that a certain figure of defence expenditure should be agreed as a first charge on the national income.

Unfortunately, however, these plans would not stand up to a situation such as arose between the wars, when the great majority of the population, and consequently all the political parties not only here, but throughout the Commonwealth and Empire, were gripped by Pacifist ideals and fell under the spell of the disarmament dream to the point of shutting their eyes to all signs of danger, and closing their ears to every note of warning. The trouble there was not national disunity, but too much unity and the lack of an opposition strong enough to bring home the dangers of an idealism that was pressed too far. Still, by providing the leaders of all parties with the facts Lord Chatfield's plans would give them the means, if they had the will, to check dangerous tendencies before they got out of hand, and with goodwill the plan should be workable.

PUBLIC OPINION

Danger is especially liable to arise again after a lapse of years, when a new generation has arisen that knew not the war. The only real check on a recurrence of our past unpreparedness is by the spread of greater knowledge and understanding among the people as to the importance of national defence.

HISTORIES AND MEMOIRS

After the last war ample material was published for this purpose. The Official Histories, running to over 45 volumes, cover nearly all aspects, but most of them, although invaluable as works of reference, are more suited to the historian and the technical student, for example, at the Imperial Defence College or the Service Staff Colleges and other training establishments for which they are essential, than to the general reader, and they make little popular appeal. Curiously enough none of them deals with the problem of Government Control in War, although on particular aspects they often shed light on the subject, and they were consulted in preparing the Lees Knowles Lectures.

Much more readable to the general public are the innumerable private memoirs, especially those of Lord Oxford and Asquith, with diary extracts, Mr Lloyd George, Mr Churchill, Lord Grey, Lord Haldane (*Before the War*), and most of the responsible statesmen and naval and military authorities both here and in foreign countries. These have been much more widely read than the Official Histories, but are mostly too long and expensive for the general public to buy. Shorter works like John Buchan's and Captain Liddell Hart's admirable histories have probably had a much wider circulation.

History, after all, depends at least as much upon human relationships and personal factors as upon the impact of events, but the former are out of place in Official Histories and more appropriate to private publications. It is to be hoped therefore that the modern tendency towards nationalisation of everything will not extend to history and that the publication of personal memoirs will be allowed as in the past, and will be subjected only to such censorship as is necessary to public safety.

THE UNIVERSITIES

Nowhere is a better balance of idealism tempered with realism to be found than in the historical works of our chairman, frequently quoted by the author in these pages, in writing and speaking on military matters. In delivering the Lees Knowles Lectures the thought frequently came to my mind whether the Universities, when the much-needed arts courses begin again, could not combine to spread, not jingoism of course, but the voice of reason and common-sense and a better understanding than existed before the war of the lessons of history in their application to Imperial Defence.

The Universities stand at the head of the educational pyramid. By their examinations, the text-books written by their experts, and the stream of their graduates to other Universities, colleges and schools of every grade throughout the Empire, they exercise in the aggregate an incalculable influence. A great opportunity would seem to lie before them. But if they are to take advantage of it they should receive all possible help and encouragement from Government Departments, including purchase of their books for official libraries.

Undergraduates also must remember that they have their responsibilities in these matters, for it is with them that the future lies. I shall never forget the dismay among our friends on the Continent, now our Allies, whom I used to meet at International Conferences, at some of the manifestations of extreme pacifism that occurred at certain British Universities in the early 'thirties. No amount of explanation would convince them that there was not something radically wrong with British public opinion.

During the war, of course, all that disappeared and University students were sound and solid with the rest of the country, and it is very important to the future that the same responsible attitude should be maintained after the war.

To sum up, no system of Government Control in War and in preparedness can provide for the safety of the country without a sound and healthy public opinion, and that depends to a great extent on a well-balanced appreciation of the lessons of history.

AN ALLEGORY

In closing this short volume I would recall for a moment a legend of Brittany, which inspired the French composer Debussy's music 'La Cathedrale Engloutie'—the Cathedral under the Sea. The opening suggests a vast expanse of sunlit sea with scarcely a ripple on the surface. Very soon a faint rumbling is heard—the first presage of a coming storm which increases until the whole firmament is swept by a hurricane with mountainous seas. Then we hear a faint suggestion of bells, solemn chant and song, which gradually rises in intensity until the whole cathedral has risen to the surface of the sea. The storm is dominated by the divine power of the holy shrine. Calm is gradually restored and the cathedral slowly disappears beneath the surface of the ocean.

That is an allegory of our system of defence. The cathedral was neglected between the wars. It was almost wrecked before it reached the surface. More than five years were needed, while the storm of war raged, before the cause of right and justice prevailed. When its work is done and it sinks once more beneath the waves we must never again allow it to fall into decay.

BIBLIOGRAPHY

The following published material has been consulted:

PARLIAMENTARY PAPERS

First Report of the War Office (Reconstitution) Committee, 1904.
First Report of the Dardanelles Commission, 1916.
The War Cabinet. Report for the year 1917 (Cmd. 9005, 1918).
Report of the Sub-Committee of the Committee of Imperial Defence on National and Imperial Defence, 1924 (Cmd. 2029).
Statements Relating to Defence, 1935 (Cmd. 4827), 1936 (Cmd. 5107), 1937 (Cmd. 5374), 1938 (Cmd. 5682), 1939 (Cmd. 5944).
The Organisation for Joint Planning, 1942 (Cmd. 6351).
Parliamentary Debates (Hansard) at all periods 1904–44.

OFFICIAL HISTORIES

Aspinall-Oglander, C. F. *Military Operations, Gallipoli*, vols. I and II. (1929.)
Corbett, Sir Julian S. *Naval Operations*, vols. I and II. (1920.)
Edmonds, Sir J. E. *Military Operations, France and Belgium*, 1914, vol. I. (1922.)
Fayle, C. E. *Seaborne Trade.* (1920.)
List of Principal Events, 1914–18.

MEMOIRS

Callwell, Sir C. E. *Field-Marshal Sir Henry Wilson, his Life and Diaries.* (1927.)
Churchill, Winston S. *The World Crisis*, 1911–18. (1923–27.)
Cooper, Alfred Duff. *Haig.* (1935–36.)
Fisher, Lord. *Memories.* (1919.)
—— *Records.* (1919.)
French, The Hon. Gerald. *The Life of Sir John French.* (1931.)
Grey of Fallodon, Lord. *Twenty-five Years*, 1892–1916. (1925.)
Haldane, Lord. *Before the War.* (1920.)
Hankey, Lord. 'The Origin and Development of the Committee of Imperial Defence' (*The Army Quarterly*, 1927).
—— 'The War Effort of the Dominions' (*The Nineteenth Century and After*, July 1943).
Lloyd George, Earl. *War Memoirs.* (1933–36.)
Ludendorff, E. *My War Memories*, 1914–18. (1919.)
Maximilian, Prince of Baden. *Memoirs.* (1928.)
Oxford and Asquith, Lord. *The Genesis of the War.* (1923.)
Robertson, Sir William. *Soldiers and Statesmen*, 1914–18. (1926.)
Spears, Sir E. L. *Prelude to Victory.* (1939.)

Printed in the United States
By Bookmasters